Seeing Light in the Cracks

How to Shift Your Consciousness and Raise Your Spiritual Awareness

Seeing Light in the Cracks © 2016 by Carter Francis

All rights reserved. No part of this book may be reproduced, distributed or transmitted in any form or by any means, without written permission from the publisher, except in the noncommercial uses permitted by copyright law.

For permission requests, contact Permissions Coordinator, sealofterspress@gmail.com

Printed in USA

ACKNOWLEDGMENTS

This book was a labor of love for me, but it wasn't easy. I've had plenty of help along the way. I owe a debt of gratitude to those that have been there for me every step of the way.

To Lori for making my dream come true.

To my friends Rob M. and Jim S., thanks for being there when I needed you most.

To the regulars of the In-Betweeners Group, who meet daily at the North Scottsdale Fellowship Club in Scottsdale, Arizona, thank you for loving me until I was able to love myself.

To the Band of Brothers, especially Dennis, Rich, Bruce, Jim and Alaska Mike, we've done it together for years now. Here's to many more years.

To my brother Joe and his family, thanks for being there for me.

To the love of my life, Anita, nothing in my life happens without you. Without your support and encouragement, this book could not have been written.

To our children Kaylan, Nick and Buster and our three granddaughters: Riley, Semler, and Bailey, you are the greatest gifts we possess.

Finally to my mother Pat and her husband Jim, thank you for never giving up on me, even though I gave you every reason to do so. You have been the rock of stability for me. I love you.

PREFACE

In 2013, the Library of Congress produced a list of the most influential books written by American authors. The list dates back to the time that we became a country. It was a short list. Of the 50 books that were named, only one of the 50 had listed the name "Anonymous" where the name of the author should have been.

When this book was first published in 1939, the author could never have imagined what was to lie ahead. The book spearheaded a movement that continues today, with active members numbering in the millions worldwide. Four more editions of this book have been released over the past 75 years and still the writer has not been named. Although a collaborative effort, the man who actually wrote the book never wanted to put himself above the other members of the organization, which he founded in 1935.

During his lifetime, Bill Wilson saw the book that he wrote, sell millions of copies. It inspired an organization to spread like wildfire around the globe, saving millions of people from a fate that no human being should suffer. Yet so few know who he was, what he stood for and why he wrote the book "Alcoholics Anonymous" in the first place.

For the people like myself who owe our very lives to the 12 Steps and corresponding principles that are outlined in this famous book, there is no written text, saving maybe the Bible, which has had a larger or more positive impact on our lives.

AA works just as well now as it ever has in saving alcoholics from themselves. The 12 Step program of recovery has also been successfully used to treat many other types of addiction over the years. I doubt that if 1000 people were selected at random, not more than 1 or 2 could recite the 12 Steps listed in the book. How sad, considering that 1 in 10 suffer from alcoholism.

The collective human ego is so driven by achievement and grandiosity, that the admission of our collective weaknesses seems like a step backwards and somehow self-defeating. It was the same in the 1930's and 40's as it is today. But the early members of AA realized that just the opposite was true...that by being honest about their shortcomings, the chances of their survival actually increased. It was the first of many paradoxes that became evident as the organization began to flourish.

To outsiders, AA is almost universally misunderstood. There is absolutely no demand of payment in order to attend. The only requirement for membership is the sincere desire to stop drinking. AA survives completely on the voluntary contributions of its members. The primary purpose of all members is to stay sober and help other alcoholics to achieve sobriety. Yet I have heard it referred to as a cult, or some sort of religious offshoot. That's nonsense.

What we do is pay forward the kindness that was shown to us when we were newcomers. We carry the message of hope, based on our own experiences. Since anonymity is the cornerstone of all of AA's traditions, the chances are good that someone you know well may be a member and you'd never know it. If by chance an AA member with many years of sobriety should identify themselves to you, ask them what keeps them sober. You'll find that the answer is always the same. They place their lives unreservedly in the hands of God, as they understand Him, and they are always looking for opportunities to be of service to others.

What would our world look like if everyone conducted their lives in the same fashion? I pray that I may live long enough to see even a glimpse of this idealistic dream, knowing full well that wishing for it will never make it so. Action is all that matters. So I've decided to share the concepts of this miraculous program with you. This book is my way of saying thank you to God and the people who came before me in Alcoholics Anonymous for saving my life.

No matter who you are, there is some magic in the 12 Steps for you. They encourage reliance on a Higher Power, honesty and service to others. Your Karma will never be better! And at the very least, you will be able to see suffering addicts and alcoholics with compassion instead of contempt. There are so many out there right now...perhaps even in your own family. I encourage you to educate yourself, because the day might come when you are the only person who can make a difference in the life of another human being. If the roles were reversed, how would you want to be treated? If that sounds familiar, that's because it is.

It's called The Golden Rule!

INTRODUCTION

A BRIEF HISTORY OF THE 12 STEPS

In 1935, a man from New York traveled to Akron, Ohio for business. He was a chronic alcoholic who had undergone several extended hospital stays in recent years in an effort to overcome his drinking problem. He hadn't had a drink in six months or so, but was on very shaky ground. At the hotel where he was staying, he came to a moment of truth. He could hear people in the hotel bar laughing and drinking. His mind started to race. He was alone far from home and the terrifying prospect of drinking again, knowing full well where it would surely lead, was back. He knew that once he started he was doomed. His last bout with the bottle had taken him to death's door.

He never took that drink. Instead, he used the telephone in the lobby to contact local hospitals and sanitariums in an effort to find someone like himself, a chronic alcoholic, to talk with. He knew that by sharing with another alcoholic, his present obsession to drink would be lifted. He was put into contact with a local doctor, a man firmly in the grips of alcoholic madness and the two men met several times in the coming days. By sharing honestly with one another about their pasts, turning their lives over to the care of God as they understood Him and searching out other alcoholics to share their ideas with, both men stayed sober. That was the humble beginning to what would ultimately become Alcoholics Anonymous. These are the men who designed the 12 Steps that we use today.

At that time, very little about alcoholism was really understood. Alcoholics were regarded as social misfits, lacking in moral fiber and willpower. Quite often they died from their disease, leaving behind heartbroken families. Doctors who treated them had few answers. Hospitals, institutions and death awaited the chronic alcoholic, with scant chance of reprieve.

The medical community and even the alcoholic himself, knew that there was some sort of disconnect in the mind of the sufferer. One doctor in particular also made mention of a bodily allergy, known in those days as the "phenomenon of craving" which is unique to the alcoholic and never manifests itself in normal drinkers...people we now refer to as "normies."

What Bill W. and Dr. Bob (the founding members and driving force behind AA) discovered was that there was a spiritual component that was essential to the recovery of any alcoholic. It had nothing to do with organized religion, although there was a heavy Christian influence in their early writings. What they learned as the fellowship of Alcoholics Anonymous began to grow, was that rigorous honesty and tireless effort to improve their spiritual condition were the keystones to their recovery.

It became understood that alcoholism was a three headed monster. It had mental, physical and spiritual components which all needed to be treated. Today, the American Medical Association recognizes alcoholism as a disease. After extensive study on the brain in recent years, there was finally confirmation that alcoholism fits the disease model. Sadly, there are still many who live in ignorance, preferring to defend a biased mindset against alcoholics, or for that matter anyone who suffers under the weight of addiction, perceiving them as weak-willed and undisciplined. This couldn't be further from the truth.

One thing that every human being is addicted to is the idea of control. It's more destructive than any drink or drug ever created. It's also the reason I decided to write this book, because it applies to all people, without exception. The spiritually-based life, which is put forth in the 12 Step program, shows us the truth about control, powerlessness and surrender. We learn to solve all of our problems on a spiritual basis, rather than trying to control outcomes ourselves.

WHAT IT MEANS FOR YOU

The 12 Step journey is simply a program for living that really works. Many believe it was divinely inspired, including myself. Although originally designed to help alcoholics, the steps have become widely accepted as a way to recover from all types of problems. More importantly, they provide a pathway to spiritual growth and a personal relationship with a God of your own understanding.

Since God is the only omnipotent being and the Creator of all things, then it stands to reason that God can be found no matter where you choose to look. Until we begin to seek God on a personal level, a spiritually based life cannot exist.

COMING TOGETHER

We have the ability to change the world we live in now more than ever. And we need to. The world is filled with broken thinking and ideology, leaving a trail of carnage in its wake. Healing begins with each individual embracing a higher standard of conduct and responsibility. This book outlines a program of action that makes this type of positive change possible.

We're hard wired with survival instincts based on genetic makeup, we achieve far more together than we can separately, we have an amazing capacity for both compassion and cruelty and are the only creatures on this planet gifted with free will. So where does that leave us since we're crowded together on this planet? You would think that resolving differences in order to make life better for everyone would be second nature. I don't see that. I see fracturing due to conflicting belief systems.

It could be argued that every war ever fought, every hate crime ever committed, or any of the other atrocities inflicted by human beings on each other can be traced back to the lack of acceptance for the right of each person to believe what they want. Shouldn't we all have that right? It's perfectly logical, since all men and women are created equally by God. We get into trouble when we start acting like we are God, trying to control the lives of others with coercion, intimidation and fear.

WHY ARE WE HERE?

During our lifetime, certain questions arise from somewhere deep inside of us and move toward the conscious mind. Why are we here? Is the path of our life just existence and survival by the best means possible, or do we have a greater purpose? Is all of this just a fortuitous cosmic anomaly, or are we a part of some Divine plan? These are questions as old as man.

There's another question that needs to be asked. Are we willing to sacrifice our happiness in order to be right? I'm not talking about correcting our children when they get out of line, or being factual about this or that. This is about forcing others to live under our control. It happens to some extent every day.

God (spirituality) and love are synonymous. Love has no boundaries and excludes no one. If you follow that line of thinking, then it's reasonable to assume that we all need love flowing in and out in both our human and spiritual interactions in order to be whole. We need to treat ourselves and each other, much better than we currently do.

We're all born with a spirit. Spirituality, therefore, is an intrinsic part of who and what we are. For people who live on a spiritual plane, the idea of being right gives way to being happy on a daily basis. If a particular religious affiliation feeds their spirit, giving them clarity and illumination, that's great. But it's not required.

What is required is an open mind, a personal relationship with God, as you understand Him and the willingness to take an unflinching look at your life, your belief system and the world you live in with an honest heart.

OUR CONNECTION TO OTHERS

Coming face to face with who and what you are (honesty) is not for the faint of heart. Asking hard questions and being willing to accept the truth about you is no easy task. Living the life that you were intended to live has direct implications on not only your family, but on every man, woman and child. Does that sound overly dramatic? It isn't.

What we do causes a ripple effect. Every action we take as individuals resembles a pebble falling in a lake. It causes a small ripple moving outward in all directions. The ripple seems to dissipate over a period of distance and time. When 6 billion pebbles (the world population) are being dropped into the same lake at the same time, over and over each day, those tiny ripples start to form something that more resembles a tsunami and at a bare minimum keep the waters in constant motion and turmoil. We frequently believe that our choices affect only us, but that couldn't be further from the truth.

We need a spiritual connection to a Higher Power of our own understanding. From this spiritual link, we get the direction and empowerment necessary to take action and become our best possible self. The source of power that we tap into is unlimited. Fear, (the driving force behind most human misdeeds) dissipates and life takes on new purpose. Without purpose, life is random and meaningless, empty and confusing. It can seem more like a life sentence than what it actually is...a gift.

You can alter the course of your life and those who come in contact with you starting now. It's a simple matter of making the decision to change and then following through with some action. You will encounter obstacles on the path to enlightenment, none larger than the preconceived notions that have lived in your own mind for decades perhaps. They can be overcome.

WHAT WE ARE UP AGAINST

There is so much interference in the world today. Distraction is more than just a nuisance. It's become a lifestyle and a dangerous one at that. It breaks our connection with what some call the "Sunshine of the Spirit", ultimately leaving us vulnerable and confused. We become cut off little by little until one day we find ourselves adrift, afraid and alone. Our lives were meant for so much more. We have a symbiotic connection to everything and everyone. The current of energy that created all things surrounds us, waiting to be tapped into.

Convinced that we have far more power and control over outcomes than we really do, we interrupt life's natural flow, stirring the pot in order to get our own way. But control is an illusion. It's the most destructive and self-sabotaging belief that we can maintain during our lifetime. We're selfish creatures. When we play God, chaos is inevitably the end result.

From birth to death, we are constantly learning and changing. The choice to fill ourselves with positive, life-affirming beliefs, which lead to positive change and true illumination, is ours alone. In order to effect change, action must be taken...and it's not always pleasant. It's work. It requires honest self-appraisal, open-mindedness and courage.

The power that's required to elevate your life to one of true freedom does not spring from human origins. It can only be obtained from a Power Greater Than Yourself. For our purposes here, I will refer to that source as God. But God goes by many names and answers all who seek Him. Don't get hung up on a name. If you struggle with the concept of God, or a Higher Power, fear not. People in AA love to say, "The hoop you have to jump through is much wider than you think!"

We are not unique from other people, no matter what our particular differences may be. That mindset of uniqueness causes separation between us and breaks the natural flow that needs to pass from person to person in order for all to flourish. What kind of life, if any, would we have now if those who had come before us, given the technology and all the advantages we enjoy, lived like we do? I shudder to think about it. These advancements have given us the keys to unlock our universe, but we can't seem to get along with our neighbors. Our pursuit of knowledge is a noble one. God gave us brains for a reason. But he also gave us feelings and a built-in compass. We refer to it as a conscience. Selfishness (also known as ego) is the only known OFF switch.

Why are we so afraid to feel? Feelings have become negatively linked with vulnerability. I believe we've been systematically conditioned to believe that vulnerability is a sign of weakness and somehow wrong. This belief could not be more wrong. When we break away from societal norms and embrace vulnerability, as the 12 Steps encourage us to do, we encounter one of life's great paradoxes. Our willingness to open up to a spiritual program of action becomes a gateway to unimaginable strength and power!

I've learned that doing the next "right" thing ultimately changes the way I think. In simpler terms, I act my way into better thinking. It's one of the basic axioms of recovery, but contrary to human logic. Action is all that really matters. When future generations look back at how we lived, our best thinking will be of little consequence to them if our actions were poor.

CHANGING OUR PERSPECTIVE

I'd like to share something I heard one day a few years back. It made sense to my head, my heart and my spirit all at the same time. A person said that the mistake that most people make is believing that they are just human beings trying to have a spiritual experience, when in fact, we are spiritual beings that have been gifted with a human experience. I had never heard what I felt inside expressed so eloquently in words. I haven't been the same person since. It's an honest statement that makes perfect sense to an honest heart.

Generally speaking, human vision is extremely myopic. Tunnel vision prevents us from looking at the bigger picture. Who can stand outside on a starry night, gazing into the heavens and really believe that they have control over anything? It's completely laughable. Our exploration and ability to see places in the universe that are totally mind blowing have taught us one immutable fact for sure though. We are but a grain of sand in a universe without limit.

Our knowledge, although far advanced from even a hundred years ago, is just as miniscule. The smartest people on Earth can only access 10-12% of their mental capacity. We know almost nothing, yet we clumsily crash through life projecting the false aura that we have all the answers not only for ourselves, but for those whose lives come in contact with our own. Surely any reasonable person can see the flawed thinking at play here.

It is my heartfelt belief that our primary purpose as living, functioning human beings is simply to love and help each other. I can make my point simply. Brokenness always brings out the best of human nature. Looking back through history, unselfish acts of mercy and brotherly love always surface when situations look the bleakest. At the most primal level, we band together and work for the common good, when we know at an instinctual level that going our separate ways would spell doom for us all.

Why is that? Could it be that we are created with a spiritual connection to all things? I believe that's true. Spiritual connection can only be broken by us. We do it every day. Gratitude is in short supply. Personal pleasure and self-aggrandizement are routinely placed above concern for the general welfare of all people. Any degree of separation placed between people because of differences, both real and perceived, is nothing short of judgement.

It's easy to embrace like-minded people. It strokes our ego and gives us the false "positive" that everything we do is right, simply because we are not alone in our thinking. In this type of bubble, personal growth is stunted and our spiritual connection is interrupted. So I challenge you to start looking for the truth about all things, beginning with yourself.

Only heartfelt honesty, open-mindedness and the willingness to be changed will rescue us from our human condition and restore us to a spiritual state. All people deserve an opportunity to flourish. Each person should be recognized for what they can do, instead of being disregarded or marginalized simply because they don't agree with us on all things. Wisdom is attained when we understand the true value of ourselves and others.

We are all God's children and have a right to be here. He has given us the gift of life to share and enjoy. This book represents my desire to be helpful to all who choose to adopt this beautiful way of life. Together, we can begin helping each other, embracing change as a good thing and working in harmony as we journey towards our best possible life.

Chapter 1

STEP ONE...WE ADMITTED WE WERE POWERLESS OVER ALCOHOL AND THAT OUR LIVES BECAME UNMANAGEABLE

HONESTY

In recovery rooms worldwide where the 12 Steps are practiced, newcomers often ask what the most important step is. The first step is first for a reason. The designers of the steps recognized the importance of rigorous honesty early on. The people who failed to recover either could not, or would not be honest with themselves. It's the foundation on which the rest of the steps were built.

For you "normies", who live a functional life free of active addiction, the need to dive into this program headfirst may not seem necessary. If you're wondering why you should invest the time and effort to do these steps, there are some questions you should ask yourself before dismissing them. Do you desire the benefits that come from living a spiritual life instead of one that is fear-based? Would you enjoy living a life where you never felt alone again? Can you believe that the answers to some questions just can't be answered by humans? Can you accept the possibility that there is something bigger and more powerful than you?

If you answered yes to one or more, I encourage you not only to read on, but to make a decision along the way to put these steps to work in your life. You have nothing to lose and everything to gain. Besides, you'll never know how your life may improve unless you try.

THE NATURE OF POWERLESSNESS AND DENIAL

The first of the 12 Steps tells us that we are powerless over people, places, things and substances. Being powerless is part of being human. It's something that we all have in common. Sometimes it takes a big measure of honesty to see how powerless we really are. We are so proficient at creating the illusions of stability and permanence, that we conveniently forget how temporary everything about life really is.

We cannot prevent our own death, or the deaths of our loved ones. We are unable to control the turbulent nature of our planet, or anything beyond it. History shows us the inevitability of change and that time is the friend of no man. Yet we waste time in a myriad of ways, under the pretense that there will always be more of it.

Powerlessness is first understood by us as children. Physically weak and unable to defend or provide for ourselves, we realize the necessity of assistance in our lives. Our first real Higher Power is our parents or those responsible to safeguard and provide for us. They teach us what they know and get us ready to live on our own when we reach adulthood. At least that's what is supposed to happen.

As we get older, we start to push the boundaries of power and control by testing them. Our brains don't fully mature until about the age of 25, but our first attempts at control come much earlier. This is also when we begin to deceive and use dishonesty as a tool. When we find a control behavior that is useful, it becomes reinforced in our mind as positive. We are essentially creatures of habit, so quite often we hold on to the things that have worked for us in the past until they stop working completely. When we refuse to believe that our habits are causing unmanageability in our life, we begin to live in denial.

Denial can only exist in an environment devoid of absolute truth. No human being is immune to it. We use justification to perpetuate denial and sometimes may be unaware that we're stuck in this pattern until it's brought to our attention by another person. In AA, we define insanity as "doing the same thing over and over, expecting a different result." Denial makes that type of insanity possible. It allows us to remain stuck in a broken belief system. Getting honest with ourselves is the only chance we have of identifying denial. Only then can we take the action required to effect change.

To be sure, there is plenty of dishonesty on display all around us. Anyone with common sense and a television set can see it. But instead of finger pointing, which solves absolutely nothing, we need to take action at a personal level. It's time to stop casually dismissing our own behavior just because the people we know, or look up to, act badly. Just because "everyone else is doing it" doesn't mean that it's OK.

We get so caught up in what others think of us, that we easily lose perspective. It's a slippery slope that reinforces dishonesty and poor action. Instead of validation from other people, we should be looking to God for what we need. Dishonesty separates us from God's love, not because it is withheld, but simply because we close ourselves off and are unable to receive it.

Many warning signs appear when we become spiritually disconnected. We become driven by selfish motives and pursuits, often becoming restless, irritable and discontented. We may fall prey to bouts of depression and become unable to control our emotions, all the while living fear-based lives. In this state, we become incapable of helping others. Ironically, the fastest way out of selfishness is service to others.

OUT OF CONTROL

We are all addicted to something, but we tend to associate the word "addict" with a person of questionable moral fiber. It may be thoughts of a junkie shooting heroin in an alley, a previously trusted employee stealing money to fund an out-of-control gambling habit, or a known alcoholic who keeps driving while intoxicated. For those with more subtle (and socially acceptable) addictions, it's easy to put some space between themselves and "those people". We need to examine the ways that we escape and the motives behind them. The closet full of secrets is a good place to look.

Our lives can become unmanageable in an instant. It's easy to see another person as the cause of our problems and maybe sometimes that is actually the case. But if we're honest, we can "play the tape" all the way back and see that we have a part to play in pretty much everything that happens in our life, good and bad. We need to see the truth as it really is and not for what we want it to be.

You will find that unmanageability doesn't require mind altering chemicals or compulsive behaviors. It requires only a flawed belief system. We repeat bad behavior and reinforce old patterns of thinking because we are defiant, resistant to change, stubborn, prideful, or whatever label you wish to put on it. No matter what you call it, it's a big problem!

We are particularly flummoxed by our feelings. Feelings in and of themselves can never hurt anyone, but how we deal with them can have catastrophic results. Our mad scramble to mask our feelings by any means possible lies at the very heart of addiction, obsession and all types of compulsive behavior. Only a limited and conflicted spiritual connection is possible amidst the turmoil of an addicted lifestyle.

Spiritual sickness is a human problem. Dishonesty is the vehicle we use to get there. I see no unmanageability in nature, or with any of God's other creatures with whom we share this planet. A tree will always be a tree and a bee will always be a bee. They and all other organisms, follow a genetic code dominated by instinct and proliferation. They are never dishonest to what they are. They don't suffer from broken thinking. Only humans do that.

COMING HOME TO ROOST

People living in America are far more at risk of dysfunction and spiritual bankruptcy than virtually any other population. Diversion has become the national pastime. Our sense of entitlement has crept into every aspect of our lives. In the last 75 years we have gone from being the world's largest producer of virtually anything, to the world's biggest consumer of everything. It's a sudden and stunning reversal.

What was once a national pride built on hard work, determination and a fundamental belief in God, has now been replaced by something far less attractive. Our arrogance and gluttony has made us a giant target for the wrath of people all over the world. We reap what we sow. What I see today is nothing short of mass denial. Here are just a few examples.

Citizens of the United States of America (4.5% of the world's population) consume 80% of the prescription narcotic drugs that are manufactured each year worldwide. You read that right. This does not include the consumption of illegal narcotics like cocaine, heroin and meth. We're also the largest consumer of those. I could write an entire book on this one subject and maybe someday I will, but the psychology behind this disturbing fact is proof that the level of dysfunction and detachment in this country is truly frightening...bordering on systemic. Got a problem? Take a pill.

We're also the fattest country on earth. Probably no other substance is used in a self-abusive manner more than food. Obesity is so prevalent here that it's become more the rule than the exception. Heart disease and diabetes rates have more than doubled in the last 25 years. Hiding and sneaking food is no different than any other addiction. Factor in disorders other than overeating like bulimia, anorexia and binge eating and the depth of the problem becomes appalling. None of these disorders have anything to do with how we look. All are perpetuated by how we feel.

As individuals, we carry more debt per capita than any citizens of any other country. We truly suffer from the disease of "MORE." We are bombarded with advertising and commercials that only perpetuate the desire to accumulate. We've been indoctrinated in the belief that somehow we deserve more than everyone else. It's what citizens of all empires have believed for centuries. It usually peaks just before the empire in question falls under its own weight. I don't believe for one minute that we are a nation of bad people. We just stopped being accountable to ourselves and to each other.

IT'S NEVER TOO LATE

When most people think about honesty, the first thing that comes to mind is telling the truth instead of lying. But this step really isn't about that. It requires us to be honest and true to ourselves. Lying to other people is nothing more than a control mechanism. When we do it, we are aiming for a specific outcome. But when we lie to ourselves and purposely avoid looking at the truth about who we are, there is almost no limit to the destruction and chaos that can be created. We can stop this insanity at any time. It will come at the cost of false pride and ego.

There is never growth without some pain. Deep-seated dishonesty is based totally in fear. The fear of growth is not what keeps us stuck in a dishonest belief system. It's the idea of facing our feelings and the inevitable pain of guilt and shame resulting from that exercise which exacerbates or fear. Every person is capable of reacting in this manner. Our survival instinct tells us that pain is not only highly uncomfortable, it's a threat.

People who have a personal relationship with God, as they understand Him, know that they are never presented with more in this life than they can handle. The admission of our powerlessness leads us directly into the loving arms of our Creator and the opportunity to endure life's challenges without ever feeling shame or feeling alone. We become encouraged to live a life that is true to the vision God has for us.

Chapter 2

STEP TWO...WE CAME TO BELIEVE THAT A POWER GREATER THAN OURSELVES COULD RESTORE US TO SANITY

HOPE

I'm a big movie buff. Every once in a while, even a town as screwed up as Hollywood gets it right. One of my favorites is "The Shawshank Redemption." In the movie, the character Andy stands wrongly convicted of the murder of his wife and her lover, sentenced to life in prison and sent to what could aptly be described as Hell on Earth. He loses much during his 20+ years in prison, but he never loses hope. It turns out to be his salvation.

I know the dictionary definition of the word "hope". It says "to wish for something with expectation." For me, real hope is much more than a word. Any time I see the word "wish", I can't help but remember something I heard my dad say over and over during my childhood. "If wishes were horses, then beggars would ride." Essentially, it means that wishing won't get you anywhere. Only action will do that.

Then we get to the word "expectation". It's a slippery slope. I've found that placing expectations on people, places and things is a setup for future resentment. Sooner or later, they will ALWAYS let you down. I wish that this fact of life wasn't so, but it happens time and time again. So with respect to all things human, my level of expectation must be seriously tempered.

PUTTING OUR HOPE WHERE IT BELONGS

When it comes to God, however, these rules don't apply. Follow along with me on this point. When we come to believe (wish) that God would restore us to sanity (right thinking), we absolutely CAN expect a good outcome...and there will be! The God of my understanding is the personification of all things good and wants the very best for me. I had to finally come to an understanding that my power, knowledge and control were almost nothing when matched with the Great Power of the Universe and I'm good with that!

Hope is realized when we come to believe that a Power greater than ourselves *could* restore us to sanity. The key word is *could*. God can do anything for us, but only if we allow it. The power of choice and free will are gifts that He endowed us with. What we do with them is up to each of us as individuals.

I've found that God communicates to me through other people and also when I meditate. Prayer is my communication to God, showing gratitude by giving thanks. When I meditate, God speaks back through my heart. Nothing I do each day is more important than quiet time with my Higher Power.

IS GOD REAL?

God either is, or He isn't. The choice to believe or not is a personal one. God cannot be proven mathematically, a fact that has kept the scientific and religious factions at odds for millennia. We have many more questions than answers, we need help and there is definitely something out there more powerful than we are that has all the answers.

God defies human logic and reason because God is not human. Science wants to know how God is possible and that's just fine. In my opinion, we should be asking why God is necessary. A definitive equation can't prove or disprove the existence of God any more than it can prove or disprove the concepts of hope and faith. Yet we see the value of both manifest themselves positively in the lives of people we know every day. So are they real? You bet they are.

God is personal to each of us and is not a "church thing". God doesn't have an address and no specific group of people have a monopoly on God's love. Be very afraid of anyone that tells you that your life and prospects for eternal life can only be guaranteed if you believe as they do. Human beings, including clergymen, who say that they definitively speak for God are completely delusional...and dangerous.

We have a limited understanding of everything, from our origins to the present day. How could anyone have the temerity to believe that they understand the Alpha and the Omega? Only a human could muster up an ego that big. I'd laugh if it wasn't so scary.

People who use their power and fortune to smooth over their own indiscretions are far less likely to reach out for God's love and mercy than a person who holds their faith up as their greatest asset. But it's not "all or nothing." There are some very good people out there who have amassed great wealth in their lives without forgetting that all of their blessings have come from God. And they give back in every conceivable way. So you can have great faith without having to give away all of your worldly possessions to do it.

This step in your transformation is all about open-mindedness and willingness. Allow for the room to grow into your relationship with the Higher Power of your own choosing. You can do that because God is all things good. However you relate with God, as you understand Him, can never be wrong. You'll find that He can easily meet and exceed any expectations you have of Him with respect to providing positive change and a new direction in your life. That's hope.

HOPELESSNESS AND TRAGEDY

What happens when hope is lost? Hopeless people either become desperate, or they give up all together. Either way, there is never a good outcome. When we place our hope and future, in the hands of other men or worldly things, trouble is never too far away. Sometimes the consequences are unimaginable. Here's a case in point:

The aftermath of WWI left the German people in a hopeless condition. With 40% unemployment, runaway inflation and things getting exponentially worse each day, the Germans became desperate. When all seemed lost, in stepped a man offering hope, a restoration of German pride and a future filled with greatness. He spoke with true conviction. They saw great passion in this man and the message he brought to them filled them with hope...in him. For a period of time, things got better. He created jobs, stabilized their economy and restored their national pride.

They were a talented and industrious people, to be sure. The quick turnaround in Germany was staggering. Surely this man that led them was something special. He was a man of action and people everywhere took note. A world that was still smarting from the horror of the "War to end all Wars" may have had reservations about the comportment of this man who led the German people, but they saw the progress being made there. Also, the thought of getting involved with the affairs of a country that they had recently been at war with seemed like a bad idea. Other nations and peoples hoped only for peace.

Misplaced hope in a man named Adolph Hitler ultimately led the German people to their ruin and cost 40 million people their lives before he committed suicide in 1945. He was the catalyst behind the most destructive war that the Earth has ever seen, the mastermind of the Holocaust and is now viewed as one of the most despised figures in human history. If no other lesson is learned here, one should never be forgotten. Placing our hope in the hands of things human and then blindly following along, is pure folly.

Our admission of powerlessness and the dilemma we face because of it, should make it easier to understand our need for a Higher Power. If not, then where is the needed power to come from? The innate sense of God that you were born with needs to be awoken. That seed of hope, no matter how small, will grow immediately, so long as your heart and mind are open. It may take a bit of time, but answers will come.

COMING TO BELIEVE

Psychic change can only be divinely inspired. Belief that a Power greater than yourself could restore you to sanity is a great start. From that humble beginning, God will reveal Himself to you in unimaginable ways. But you need always to remember that it is your responsibility to seek God out.

God is not a bully. Although he loves each of us equally (He has no grandchildren!), he set us free in this world knowing that some would never return to Him. He doesn't force Himself on those that reject Him. We were given the gift of free will for a reason. Instead, He waits patiently for us to seek Him. When we do, we are bestowed with a multitude of gifts. None of them can be bought or sold. There is a quiet peace that grows within us, knowing that at no time will we ever again be alone. When we open the door to the idea of a loving God, He is there.

"Coming to believe" is a process that you must work your way through alone. No one can do it for you. Although some embrace this idea faster than others, there is no chance that God will forget about you. Don't hold yourself back. Fear is the only barrier to a spiritual life. God knows no fear and your own unreasonable fears will evaporate as you give yourself over to the antidote that He offers in great measure...LOVE!!!

I had an unhealthy image of God for many years. I was offered some simple advice from someone I admire greatly. He told me to write down on a piece of paper exactly what I needed God to be in my life in order for me to surrender with no reservations. He promised me that God would exceed my expectations. He was right.

You see, it worked because I began to see God as I understand Him. He was personal to ME. Needless to say, He has shown Himself to be more than I could have imagined. The fact is, I underestimated God. I always tried to relate on a human level with One who is not human. Once I was willing to let go of all my preconceived notions, a new picture of God started to take shape...one that actually made sense. You can have that too.

The God of your understanding offers an unlimited supply of love and hope. God is also the eternal source of power. God gives us what we need to get through each day and the difficult times that life is sure to throw at us. A spiritual life enables us to get in harmony with all things and become part of life, instead of being detached and apart from it.

Many of us grew up in a church environment. Some are still immersed in it and some are not. Some grew up with little or no concept of a Higher Power. No matter which group you fall into, it makes little difference. Finding your own concept of God is only a matter of opening yourself up to try.

Oddly enough, those who grew up with absolutely no exposure to organized religion may have an easier time finding a Higher Power, simply because they have no preconceived notions to overcome. They are a clean slate and open to the idea of a God that places no conditions on them in order to receive unconditional love. Those of us who grew up with organized religion were taught how we should think about God and what was mandated in order to be acceptable in God's eyes.

Either way, we need to open ourselves up to the Truth. We know nothing about God except a few things. He is, was and always will be. He loves us unconditionally. He never leaves us. It's us who leave Him. And he has a plan for each of us that is far greater than anything that we can envision for ourselves. When we open the door to the possibility of Him, God begins to fill in all of the spaces around us.

Carter Francis

Chapter 3

STEP THREE...WE MADE A DECISION TO TURN OUR WILL AND OUR LIVES OVER TO THE CARE OF GOD AS WE UNDERSTOOD HIM

FAITH

Now is the time to get off the fence and make a decision and it's a big one. Honesty has helped us see powerlessness and unmanageability in our lives. From there, Hope led us to believe that a Power greater than ourselves could restore us and enrich our lives in every way. But this isn't sufficient to effect the type of change that we're looking for. We need to make a decision to turn our will and our very lives over to this entity of Love.

So what does it mean to do that? First, it means that we begin to listen, not to the voice in our head, but rather the voice in our heart. God lives there. We stop questioning heartfelt feelings. We don't just think about doing the next "right" thing...we do it. We stop praying selfishly for ourselves. And above all, we give thanks to our Higher Power for ALL things.

Our selfishness knows no boundaries. When things are going well, how often do we see God as the reason for it, when we're breaking our arms trying to pat ourselves on the back? Too often it's only when we are in dire straits that we cry out for God to save us. We have extremely one-sided relationships, if any, with God. He gets little or no credit when things are good and all the blame when things go wrong. But He can take it.

We falsely believe that through the power of our own will, we can overcome anything. We put ourselves first, convinced of our own importance. We forget that we're here today doing life only because God wills it. There are no coincidences. There is purpose behind all things and that purpose comes from Him. All things flow in our direction, not out from our location.

LEARNING TO SURRENDER

Making a decision like this means nothing if it doesn't pass the test of time. Time is the only true measure of anything. The days of waffling back and forth on the God question must end for good and all. I like to use the term "jump the broom" when describing a leap of faith, because I don't see it as some intimidating or dangerous hurdle. It's the right thing to do. What makes it effective and lasting in the end however, is taking daily action to reinforce our decision. Faith without works is dead, dead, dead.

To say that you've given yourself over totally to a loving God and then to actually live your life in service to that belief, are two very different things. God doesn't care what you say. He cares what you do. That's the true test of faith. In the end, the footprints that we leave in our wake tell the real story of our life and how we lived it. The road to Hell really is paved with good intentions...followed by nothing.

Making a decision to implement faith into your life is positive action. It's the beginning of many more action steps on the road to enlightenment. When you perform positive actions again and again, they begin to reinforce each other, gradually becoming a functioning part of your mind.

This book is only a catalyst to start taking action. Nothing changes if nothing changes. For some of us, there have been decades dominated by broken thinking, with little or no positive action to effect change.

Transformation usually doesn't happen overnight. But it will happen if you work for it.

Although we need a spiritual awakening and a Higher Power to guide us in our daily life, the only people who receive these gift are those that really want them and are willing to go to any lengths to get them. A faith based life isn't always easy and now seems to be the road less traveled. It takes great courage to change.

People in 12 Step recovery are taught to live a program of attraction rather than promotion. When you get in line with God's will for you, people will notice. They may actually see it before you do and ask what's changed about you. Your true friends will appear and the acquaintances will fall away. You'll have opportunities to pay the gift forward when the time is right. That's a topic for a later chapter.

THE PARADOX

For now, we stay focused on downsizing our own ego. I like to say that ego is an acronym for Easing God Out! There's no room for God in our life when we believe we're in control of everything. Surrendering ourselves to something we can't see is where we encounter the ultimate paradox of our life. We surrender to win. It's radical spiritualism.

Surrender is a word that's had a nasty stigma attached to it. These days, it infers weakness and clearly defines the "loser" of any conflict. But I've learned a different definition of surrender in recent years. My friend taught me that surrendering meant joining the winning side. I guess it's all about how you look at it! I'd been fighting for years to defend a losing hand. All I had to do was lay it down in order to receive another one, a better one, one that would alter the course of my life.

As I said before, I've met scores of people in the rooms of AA that would never have occupied the same social circles. Although they represent every social strata and occupation, all were once hopeless drunks. Yet today, many are pillars of their community, great family people and selfless in their service to others. All of them give credit to a Power Greater Than Themselves and turn their will and life over to the care of this God of their understanding on a daily basis. It's the common factor in their recovery. So I see God working in the lives of others every day. What more proof do I need?

GETTING OUT OF SELF

For some, it takes great pain and suffering before encountering God's love. Only later do they discover that He was there all along, propping them up and keeping them alive. The barrier to faith was and always will be, self. The manifestations of self will always defeat us in the end.

The happiest people I know are those that have reached a place of acceptance in their lives. Peace and serenity are a choice and they understand that. The realization that we really aren't in control of outcomes is the path to acceptance. We stop playing God and start to do our part, the best that we can.

I love the Prayer of Serenity. It goes like this..."God, grant me the serenity to accept the things I cannot change, courage to change the things I can and the wisdom to know the difference." I offer this prayer up many times each day and it has saved me in moments when my patience has been severely tested. Yes, it still happens!!!

Any time I think I'm right and try to impose my beliefs on you with the expectation that you'll fall in line with my will, I'm playing God. It always leaves one party defeated and the other with a hollow victory and an even more inflated sense of self. God is nowhere to be found in such an exchange. Nobody wins.

When we turn our will and our lives over to the care of God, what can we expect? God wants the best of things for all of us, but does that mean we'll suddenly be gifted a new house or car, that all of our wants will magically manifest themselves in our lives? Hardly. But we will get exactly what we need. John Lennon wrote, "All You Need Is Love." I believe he was right.

GAINING PERSPECTIVE

God provides us with an abundance of perspective when we surrender to Him. With love in our hearts, all things fall into place. With love we gain perspective. Rudyard Kipling's' famous poem "If" beautifully describes the value of perspective.

It speaks to the fleeting and fragile nature of life. *Google* it up sometime and read it through in its entirety. Not a word is wasted or a thought unfinished. I saw the poem for the first time as a laminated copy tacked to my brother's refrigerator. I was dumbfounded when I read it. I still am amazed every time I read it.

It's hard to pick out a favorite passage from this masterpiece, but for me it's the stanza about meeting with triumph and disaster and treating those two imposters just the same. That is some fabulous advice. The ebb and flow and highs and lows of life are all temporary. Only God and our souls (spirituality) are eternal.

Before you move on, ask God for the resolve to live your life with Him at your side, guiding your thoughts and actions. There is plenty of work still to do and we'll need the help of our Higher Power to do it.

For the last 80 years, alcoholics have been saying a simple prayer to help us achieve this. Notice that the world "alcohol" is nowhere to be found! This prayer is for all people.

It's called the 3rd Step Prayer, and is found in Chapter 5 of the book Alcoholics Anonymous. You can read it on the next page.

God, I offer myself to thee, to build with me and do with me as you wilt.

Relieve me of the bondage of self, that I may better serve thy will.

Take away my difficulties, that victory over them may bear witness to those I would help of thy power, thy love and thy way of life.

May I do thy will always!

Chapter 4

STEP FOUR...WE MADE A SEARCHING AND FEARLESS MORAL INVENTORY OF OURSELVES

COURAGE

Someone much wiser than I am said that there are only two kinds of business...my business and none of my business! Why didn't I think of that? And, what does that have to do with courage? As it turns out, it has everything to do with it. Let me explain with a nugget of truth I received from a woman I admire greatly. "I can't change the truth about my past and I can't change you."

When we try to direct the rest of the world how to think and act, are we really doing God's will? No way! There are few people more despicable than hypocrites. They love to point out the faults in others, while secretly committing the same (or worse) acts themselves!

In the Gospel of Matthew, Chapter 7:1-5, the insanity of hypocrisy is exposed. Whether you have Christian beliefs or not, this just makes sense.

> "Judge not, that ye be not judged. For with what judgment ye judge, ye shall be judged: and with what measure ye mete, it shall be measured to you again. And why beholdest thou the mote that is in thy brother's eye, but considerest not the beam that is in thine own eye?

> *Or how wilt thou say to thy brother, Let me pull out the mote out of thine eye; and, behold, a beam is in thine own eye? Thou hypocrite, first cast out the beam out of thine own eye; and then shalt thou see clearly to cast out the mote out of thy brother's eye."*

In plain English, it simply says we should quit pointing out the twig that is lodged in someone else's eye when we have a log stuck in our own! We need to keep our own house clean. What we do matters. And what we've done matters also. Although we can't change the past, we need to face it as it really was and not how we wish it would have been.

TAKING INVENTORY OF OURSELVES

People who disregard history and the lessons to be learned by it, are doomed to repeat it. Since our objective is to be scrubbed clean and change from the inside out, we need to take a hard, honest look at how we arrived at today. Dwelling on the past in some morbid way is not the goal here, but we need to complete a thorough inventory identifying our greater deficiencies. We all have them. Sometimes they are known to others and sometimes they are secrets that we keep inside...fearful of what their exposure may subject us to. Either way, they need to be looked at fearlessly. Now you know why this chapter is called "Courage".

We face many obstacles in our lives, none bigger than ourselves. Our capacity to deceive ourselves and others is stupefying. Fooling others with our trickery and lies is never a good thing, but living in denial and lying to ourselves in order to perpetuate a dysfunctional belief system is tantamount to spiritual suicide. It's a BIG deal.

Some have more baggage than others. It all needs to be looked at and understood. We must examine the motives behind our past action and see our part in every encounter. We look at people, places and things that have caused us to be resentful. We write down everything we can remember about how we felt at those times and how we reacted.

In time, we come to see how we had a part to play in everything that ever happened to us. There are few exceptions. No matter how painful it may feel, we avoid nothing. Remember, as awful as points of your past may have been, they didn't kill you. You're still here. Your freshly reinforced principles of Honesty, Hope and Faith will give you the courage necessary to look at the past objectively.

We simply cannot avoid this step in our transformation. The past can hold great power over us. Obviously, it has helped shape our lives to this point and can have direct bearing on the course of future decisions and events. Often times we learn much more from moments we would just as soon forget than anything else.

Secrets have the power to kill, so we need to expose them to the Light and then let them go. Like resentments, they are poison for the soul and keep us living in various states of fear. I can't overstate how dangerous this is. People who are filled with unhealthy fears are susceptible to all kinds of crazy thoughts and behaviors.

If you've never done a written inventory, then it's time to start. This requires action and some time. Everything looks different on a piece of paper. Writing it all down takes the power out of it, giving us the objectivity to see the facts...no more and no less. Truth is our only objective. It enables us to identify the character defects that impede our spiritual development.

Getting started on an inventory is often difficult for people who aren't already in the habit of journaling, but the first part of our inventory consists of something that we all carry around...resentments. It's easy for us to bring forward the images of people who have wronged us throughout our lives. So we start there. We make a list, going back as far as we can remember, of people and institutions that angered and offended us, then list the grievances we have against them in a column beside their name.

The resentment part of the inventory is critical for us. Resentments are powerful motivators for all types of insane behavior. When we point our resentments outward, it's not just the object of our outrage that feels the wrath. People who may have absolutely nothing to do with either party can be affected in tragic ways. When we carry forth anger, due to a particular resentment we are harboring, our judgement is affected. Have you ever driven a car when you were fuming mad about something? You get the idea.

People carry resentments for years over cheating spouses, being passed over for a promotion that they actually deserved, or things along those lines. Think about this though. While you burn your tormentors in effigy in your mind for years, wishing pain and eternal damnation on them for being bottom feeding scumbags, are these thoughts actually having any effect on them? Doubtful. All you've really done is give these people that hurt you free rent in your head, while keeping yourself locked in a prison of misery and self-destruction.

"Stuffing" our feelings is the breeding ground for all types of addictive behavior. Anything we do excess in order to distract ourselves from what we feel has potentially fatal consequences. The types of addictive behavior we engage in is staggering. Although drugs (both legal and illegal) and alcohol get much of the focus, we can easily add shopping, gambling, eating disorders, video gaming and sex as addictions that swallow the souls of people in pain. This short list of vices barely scratches the surface. Again we see why honesty with ourselves is paramount. What do you do to hide from your feelings (make yourself feel better)?

GOD SAVE ME FROM ANGER

Whether your response to resentment manifests itself in retaliatory actions directed at others, or if your destructive tendencies point inward, I think we can agree that resentment is a double-edged sword. There are no winners. We must be free of them in order to be happy and truly free.

Several years ago, I came across something written by a man named Frederick Buechner. It illustrates the broken thinking that occurs when deep resentment is allowed to take hold.

> *Of the 7 Deadly Sins, Anger is possibly the most fun. To lick your wounds, to smack your lips over grievances long past, to roll over your tongue the prospect of bitter confrontations still to come, to savor to the last toothsome morsel both the pain you are given and the pain you are giving back -- in many ways it is a feast fit for a King. The chief drawback is that what you are wolfing down is yourself. The skeleton at the feast is YOU!!!*

So what is the antidote for bitter resentment? *Forgiveness.* In the past you may have sworn secretly that you'd rather die before "lowering yourself" far enough to try it. Guess what? You might. But it's the only way out.

Forgiveness is the master of resentment. It works when nothing else does, but our ego and pride don't like it one bit. Being able to forgive transgressions, no matter how heinous, is the key we use to release ourselves from Hell and walk unburdened into the Light. It's a simple concept, but not always easy.

So far, we've listed the people and institutions that we feel have wronged us, adjacent to the specifics of the transgression. For many of us, this is as far as we ever get. But we need to go farther. So we identify the feelings that these actions raised in us. When we get right down to it, fear usually lies at root of our feelings. We fear abandonment, financial ruin, threats to us physically and all other types of scary future possibilities due to the action of others.

Finally, we need to write down what part, if any, we played in all of these instances. If we're honest, we'll be able to see that we indeed had some influence in every single thing that's happened to us in our adult lives. We always tend to minimize our part, no matter how significant, getting only far enough to see the other party or parties as "more wrong." Honesty is sometimes a lonely path. Write it down.

Intimate relationships are always a hot spot for resentments. Why? Because we have expectations that we level on the people closest to us. Expectations are just future resentments waiting to happen. Think about it. Usually this happens when communication breaks down. We take for granted that the special people in our lives will always do our bidding, only because it's what we want and expect. Really?

I prefer to live my life with little or no expectation of any other person. I have choices. If I find things unacceptable, I can either leave it alone or deal with it...but either way it's my choice. I just have to accept what the outcome of my decision proves to be. So I pray that God will direct my thinking with respect to relationships and give me the gift of "pause". My natural reaction when things don't go my way is never good, but when I choose not to engage and ask for guidance, things usually go much better.

The tongue is a well-honed sword. We've all been cut to the bone with harsh words. Once words leave our mouth, we can't get them back. I harken back to the saying that we all heard as children. *If you can't say something nice, don't say anything at all*. It costs absolutely nothing (except sometimes our pride) to stay quiet when provoked, or disarm someone with a kind word.

When I did this step thoroughly, I had over 40 pages filled on both sides. Needless to say, I had issues! But after I finished and looked at it objectively with a trusted friend, I saw the path that took me to the lowest point in my life. The world and everyone in it had been dominating me for decades, but you never would have heard me admit it. I had a massive ego, was convinced that I could handle everything myself and fell victim to an untenable belief system that almost killed me. AA's describe themselves as egomaniacs with an inferiority complex. Believe me when I say that alcoholics don't have a corner on that market! They're just honest enough to admit it.

DON'T FORGET ABOUT SEX

You may have raised an eyebrow when you read the part about getting help from another person. Exposing our life to someone else can cause some huge anxiety. We all have trust issues, some more than others. But we need the objective view of a trusted friend or counselor to ask the hard questions and then listen without judgement. Do not do this with your spouse or significant other!!! Here's why.

We can't do a thorough inventory without looking at past sexual behavior. This information could have some explosive repercussions if it were to fall into the wrong hands, but we absolutely cannot look the other way because we're uncomfortable.

Perhaps nothing motivates us more than the drive to reproduce. It's an intrinsic part of who we are. Oftentimes, our sexual urges have overridden good judgement, causing all sorts of problems. Each of us have a comfort level with past and present sexual behavior. If there instances in your past that are troublesome to you, write them down. We're looking at the motives behind what we've done and nothing more.

Sexual preferences are matters for the individual and not relative here. If we hurt someone because of selfish desires or lied to them in order to get what we want, we need to examine it. We go to any lengths to find the truth about who we are. God gives us the courage and strength to look at everything.

JUST DO IT

All of the information we gather during this process is extremely valuable. What we learn here has direct correlation with all future steps. You'll see why as we move forward. So a "searching and thorough moral inventory" is just that.

There are people out there who can help you with this step. Counselors, therapists and religious leaders are quite familiar with the 12 Step model. They are also bound to confidentiality, so those of you with trust issues can breathe easier. Now if you have a close-mouthed friend with experience in step work who you prefer to do this with, that's great. In AA, people with more time in the program typically "sponsor" newcomers who are doing these steps for the first time, taking them through all 12 just as someone had done for them previously. We pay it forward.

Try not to get caught up in being perfect. It can't be done. Be honest with yourself and do the work to the best of your ability. Life is good and it's about to get a whole lot better!!!

Chapter 5

STEP FIVE...WE ADMITTED TO GOD, TO OURSELVES AND TO ANOTHER HUMAN BEING THE EXACT NATURE OF OUR WRONGS

INTEGRITY

God gives us grace on an industrial scale. Grace is defined as "the unmerited love and favor of God towards man." We need to meet that type of love with a simple gift of our own. Confessing our shortcomings is truly graceful, no matter how awkward it may feel to us. I believe wholeheartedly that it pleases God immensely when we do. Have you ever heard the story of "The Prodigal Son"? Just like in the parable, when we return to Our Father (God), there is great celebration and joy, regardless of the mistakes we've made.

An honest and complete accounting needs to be our choice. This admission provides relief and the desire to be a better person. This act may also lead to our first direct encounter with God's love, or for that matter, God Himself. Also, we gain a measure of integrity by working through this exercise, building on it for the rest of our lives.

CONFESSION IS GOOD FOR THE SOUL

Integrity is embodied in people who are unimpaired, have an air of soundness to them and live by a code of strict personal honesty. Does that sound like you? If you fall short of the mark and most people do, don't worry. God doesn't make trash.

The true value of this step is found in the act itself and not in the amount and nature of our despicable deeds. When we empty ourselves of the poisonous past, the world doesn't change...but we do. Confession really is good for the soul. My experience with this step is not unlike the accounts of many others who reported feeling like they could float upon completion of their admission.

An informed and enlightened mind will adapt to a more merciful and understanding system of justice. This step takes us in that direction for sure. Our own restoration is a gateway to understanding others, hopefully motivating us to reach out and assist them in their own spiritual elevation. Acceptance of self, with all of our faults, gradually pushes out the habits of self-abuse and our perspective about everything begins to change.

OPENING OURSELVES UP TO ANOTHER PERSON

This is a critical step in recovery. If we fail to tell all, the joyful life of peace and serenity will elude us. What holds most people back is the idea of telling their deepest, darkest secrets to another person. Few things in life will ever leave us more exposed and vulnerable. But that's exactly why we do it. It takes plenty of humility, faith and courage to "man up" and put it all on the table.

Giving a thorough accounting of our past to another person makes us accountable to the entire human race. It bridges the divide that we alone have placed between ourselves and the rest of the world. In our efforts to protect ourselves, we have systematically erected barrier after barrier around us. We've all done it.

We are all sinners in the eyes of God. It's unavoidable...and God knows that. He has forgiven us all of our transgressions even before we acted. We need to remember that when facing this step. There are no big deals!

Even so, it is always prudent to do this step with a close-mouthed friend or a professional in whose confidentiality you can depend on.

What is said between the two of you is for your ears only. Most people who refuse to admit their sins out loud do so because of the possible consequences that may befall them were the information to ever be made public. Again, this is an attempt to control outcomes, meaning that reliance and faith in God are still not fully manifested. We need to find someone that we trust and let it all go!

GETTING OVER OLD IDEAS

Richard Rohr, acclaimed author and Franciscan priest, wrote about the "economy of grace" in his book "Breathing Under Water". He masterfully walks the reader through this concept in the following paragraph.

> *"The revelation from the cross and the Twelve Steps, however, believes that sin and failure are, in fact, the setting and opportunity for the transformation and enlightenment of the offender--and then the future will take care of itself. It is a mystery that makes sense to the soul and is entirely an 'economy of grace' which makes sense only to those who have experienced it."*

If that seems hard to believe or understand, don't worry about it. If you are thorough and admit the exact nature of your wrongs, you'll understand it perfectly when you're done. This isn't about crime and punishment. It's about transformation and redemption.

The system of control, or what Rohr calls "retributive justice", has been in effect for thousands of years. And it's broken. It mandates that a person can only repent and transform after they've been punished for a sin. Obviously, the lessons available from the life and death of Jesus have been completely ignored. No wonder our prisons are overcrowded and the recidivism rate is so high.

God meets everything, including sin, with unconditional love, thereby eliminating the need for punishment when we confess honestly and completely. When met with God's love and grace, we transform immediately and repent with action from that point forward. This is called "restorative justice". And it really works!

The 12 Steps are all about the necessity of change. I said in an earlier chapter that we are spiritual beings having a human experience. The 5th Step is a spiritual exercise designed to get us out of our human shackles for good. Although we do this in the presence of another person, God's presence will be clearly felt throughout. The verbalization of our life's story may take hours, or even days. But God will never leave, never punish and never withdraw that unconditional love that He clearly shows to us all.

There is no reason to fear this step. Fear is for people without faith. Your God has given you everything. Now it's your turn to give it back and return to Him with your whole heart and soul. You were given a clean slate as you entered this world. This step is the opportunity to have it wiped clean all over again, maybe for the first time in your life. It's a deeply emotional experience, one you do not want to deprive yourself of.

Finally, an understanding needs to be reached both mentally and spiritually that every life has value. In the eyes of God, there is no favor granted on some sort of merit system. This erroneous belief has been perpetuated by human beings alone, for the strict purpose of holding power and authority over others. The old dualistic system, which promulgates class systems, the abuse of religious authority and moral superiority over other human beings, needs to be retired once and for all.

Doing an honest 5th Step will give you more than just a glimpse of the possibilities that lie beyond the human entanglements that have held you bound for so long. It will open your mind and heart. Your life will be recognizable to you as the gift that it is. You will know freedom and love in great measure. But we don't stop here...there is yet more to do.

Carter Francis

Chapter 6

STEP SIX...WE WERE ENTIRELY READY TO HAVE GOD REMOVE ALL THESE DEFECTS OF CHARACTER

WILLINGNESS

How do we shed a lifetime of character defects? We can't, if left to our own devices. But what we can do is become willing to let God remove them all. To offer ourselves without hesitation, deferring to God's wisdom and love for us, is a huge step. We let God drive the bus. He knows the direction that our lives should move in. He knows what we need and when we need it. Our job is to make ourselves ready to follow the path that God lays out for us.

People find their way back to this step again and again. It takes a great level of commitment to surrender completely. I believe that anyone is capable of releasing control to Him for short periods of time. But the willingness to defer to our Higher Power each day of our life takes commitment. When we get caught up in the ebbs and flows of life, old patterns try to re-emerge. Our character defects spring back into action, driven by our need to regain control. As painful as it may be, we learn each time we backslide and the old, comfortable tapes begin to play in our head. Through trial and error, we learn to stop struggling. God never intended for us to solve our problems alone.

RELAX AND TRUST GOD

There is a children's toy called Chinese handcuffs. For those unfamiliar with them, they are nothing more than a woven tube that encases a finger from each hand, essentially binding the hands together. The harder you pull and twist your fingers apart in an effort to free yourself, the tighter it becomes on your fingers. Only when you stop struggling and relax, making slow and deliberate movements while controlling your breathing, perspiration and blood pressure, can you free yourself. Ultimately, the bind loosens and falls away. It's a valuable lesson.

When thinking about character defects, it's important to understand what they are. Usually fear based, they are warped versions of the God-given instincts that we were all born with, instincts that are inherently good. We need to keep in mind that character defects, regardless of how much we may dislike them, come with the territory. We wouldn't be human without them.

Any expectations we may have that our shortcomings will vanish completely are unreasonable. God gives us the grace to be perfectly imperfect. We must come to the understanding that we don't know what's best for us. That's why we offer all of our character defects to Him. We allow God to fit us into life each day, with or without certain character defects, in order to best do His will. Certain character defects may be useful in order to carry that out. That sounds confusing, but consider this. How are we to be helpful to another person if they can't identify with us? Without character defects, we would be unrecognizable to other people!

Our Higher Power knows everything about us. There is no hiding. And really no reason to hide in the first place. If God was going to strike us down with vengeance (a human character defect) every time we weren't perfect, there wouldn't be a single one of us left! The gift of human life is just that...a gift from God. He knows that we will struggle and sometimes fail. He allows us to wake up each day with our humanity and character defects, in tow. The choice to turn to Him for help is up to us.

THE NATURE OF THE BEAST

Our defects of character are as comfortable as skin. If they weren't, we would have tried to shed them long ago. We wear different masks, adopting the persona that allows us to have our way. Selfishness is the root of our problem. We like to hold onto things we deem to be "ours". To be willing to have God remove any and every defect of character is, as my friends in AA like to say, "what separates the men from the boys." Believe it.

If you are still unclear what character defects look like, then the following list should provide some clarity. Take an honest look and mark any that apply. Even if you can only remember doing a specific thing once, it still counts. It shows what you're capable of, both good and bad.

CHARACTER DEFECT		OPPOSITE ASSET
Aggressive, Belligerent	→	Good-natured, Gentle
Angry	→	Forgiving, Calm Gentle
Apathetic	→	Interested, Concerned, Alert
Apprehensive, Afraid	→	Calm, Courageous
Argumentative, Quarrelsome	→	Agreeable
Arrogant, Insolent	→	Unassuming, Humble
Attacking, Critical	→	Fair, Self-restrained

CHARACTER DEFECT		OPPOSITE ASSET
Avoidant	→	Faces problems and acts
Blocking	→	Honest, Intuitive
Boastful	→	Modest, Humble
Careless	→	Careful, Painstaking, Concerned
Cheating	→	Honest
Competitive (socially)	→	Cooperative
Compulsive	→	Free
Conceited, Self-important	→	Humble, Modest
Contradictory, Oppositional	→	Reasonable, Agreeable
Contrary, Intractable, Pigheaded	→	Reasonable
Controlling	→	Letting go, especially of others lives
Cowardly	→	Brave

CHARACTER DEFECT		OPPOSITE ASSET
Critical	→	Non-judgmental, Praising, Tolerant
Cynical	→	Open-minded
Deceitful	→	Guiltless, Honest
Defensive	→	Open to criticism
Defiant, Contemptuous	→	Respectful
Denying	→	Honest, Accepting
Dependent	→	Accepts help but is self-reliant
Depressed, Morose	→	Hopeful, Optimistic, Cheerful
Dirty, Poor Hygiene	→	Clean
Dishonest	→	Honest
Disloyal, Treacherous	→	Faithful, Loyal
Disobedient	→	Obedient

CHARACTER DEFECT		OPPOSITE ASSET
Disrespectful, Insolent	→	Respectful, Reverent
Enabling	→	Setting Boundaries, Tough Love
Envying	→	Empathetic, Generous, Admiring
Evasive	→	Candid, Straightforward
Exaggerating	→	Honest, Realistic
Faithless	→	Reliable, Faithful
Falsely Modest	→	Honest, Has Self-esteem
Falsely Modest	→	Modest, Humble
Fantasizing, Unrealistic	→	Practical, Realistic
Fearful	→	Confident, Courageous
Forgetful	→	Responsible
Gluttonous, Excessive	→	Moderate

CHARACTER DEFECT		OPPOSITE ASSET
Gossiping	→	Closed-mouthed, Kind, Praising
Greedy	→	Moderate, Generous, Sharing
Hateful	→	Forgiving, Loving, Concerned for others
Hypersensitive	→	Tolerant, Doesn't Personalize
Ill-tempered, Bitchy	→	Good-tempered, Calm
Impatient	→	Patient
Impulsive, Reckless	→	Consistent, Considers Ramifications
Inconsiderate	→	Thoughtful
Indecisive, Timid	→	Firm, Decisive
Indifferent, Apathetic, Aloof	→	Caring
Inflexible, Stubborn	→	Open-minded
Insecure, Anxious	→	Self-confident

CHARACTER DEFECT		OPPOSITE ASSET
Insincere, Hypocritical	→	Sincere, Honest
Intolerant	→	Understanding, Patient
Irresponsible, Reckless	→	Responsible
Isolating, Solitary	→	Sociable, Outgoing
Jealous	→	Trusting
Judgmental	→	Open-minded, Tolerant
Lazy, Indolent	→	Industrious
Loud	→	Tasteful, Reserved
Lustful	→	Healthy Sexuality
Lying	→	Honest
Manipulative	→	Candid, Honest, Non-controlling
Masked, Closed	→	Honest, Open, Candid

CHARACTER DEFECT		OPPOSITE ASSET
Nagging	→	Supportive
Obscene, Crude	→	Modest, Courteous
Perfectionistic	→	Realistic Goals
Pessimistic	→	Hopeful, Optimistic, Trusting
Possessive	→	Generous
Prejudiced	→	Open-minded
Procrastinates	→	Disciplined, Acts Promptly
Rationalizing	→	Being Honest
Resentful, Bitter, Hating	→	Forgiving
Resistant	→	Willing
Rude	→	Polite, Courteous
Sarcastic	→	Praising, Tolerant

CHARACTER DEFECT		OPPOSITE ASSET
Self-important	→	Humble, Modest
Self-destructive	→	Self-fulfilling
Self-pitying	→	Grateful, Realistic, Accepting
Self-righteous	→	Humble, Understanding
Self-seeking	→	Selfless, Concerned for Others
Selfish	→	Altruistic
Shy	→	Outgoing
Spiteful	→	Forgiving
Stubborn	→	Willing
Sullen	→	Cheerful
Superior, Grandiose	→	Humble
Superstitious	→	Realistic

CHARACTER DEFECT		OPPOSITE ASSET
Suspicious	→	Trusting
Tense	→	Calm, Serene
Thinking Negatively	→	Staying Positive
Treacherous	→	Trustworthy
Unfair	→	Fair
Ungrateful	→	Thankful
Useless	→	Helpful
Vain	→	Modest, Humble
Vindictive	→	Forgiving
Violent	→	Gentle
Vulgar	→	Polite
Wasteful	→	Thrifty

CHARACTER DEFECT		OPPOSITE ASSET
Withdrawn	→	Outgoing
Wordy, Verbose	→	Frank, To the point, Succinct

The origin of this list is unknown. It's been passed between people in recovery for decades. There are a couple of things about it that stand out. First, the words honest and humble appear numerous times on the asset side. How honest and humble is the world you live in today and what can you do about it? All that any of us can do is live an honest and humble life as an example to others. People emulate what they see every day.

The second and perhaps less obvious thing I see, is that FEAR of some sort is behind every character defect, while LOVE fuels every asset. It's easy to see where the path of least resistance lies. Unreasonable and unhealthy fears can only live and grow in an environment devoid of God.

To become willing and then to eventually stay willing to have God remove all of our character defects, is a growth process. If you become just a little bit more willing tomorrow than you are today, then you're headed in the right direction. The process begins with awareness.

PLUGGING IN

Prayer and meditation are the best ways to maintain our connection with God, which in turn strengthens our symbiotic relationship with everything else. A simple prayer each morning to have God direct us towards balanced thinking is a great start. It opens our heart and mind to God's will and elevates us spiritually. Most importantly, we go out into the world with the knowledge that we are not alone. It's amazing how much better we act when we are aware of God's presence throughout the day.

Some quiet time in the evening for reflective meditation helps us gain perspective. Life happens on life's terms. It's so easy to get caught up in it all, sending us on a roller coaster of emotions. Meditation is an opportunity to recharge while waiting patiently for God's message. A moment of pause is an opportunity to reflect on our blessings and with all the negativity that we are bombarded with in society today, having an attitude of gratitude gives us the balance we need to keep moving forward.

God loves us, imperfections and all. And if He loves us despite our character flaws, then shouldn't we be a bit easier on ourselves? If we're willing to let God have His way, anything becomes possible. God delights in taking the most broken of people, making them whole again and then using them as examples for everyone to follow. Looking back through history, we see that His "reclamation projects" have become some of the world's great leaders. They stand as beacons of hope for those who struggle and aspire to a better life and world in which to live it. God doesn't call the qualified...He qualifies the called!

Carter Francis

Chapter 7

STEP SEVEN...WE HUMBLY ASKED HIM TO REMOVE OUR SHORTCOMINGS

HUMILITY

What does it mean to be humble? By the time we get to this step, we should have a pretty good idea. Humility lies at the foundation of every step we take on our road to recovery and enlightenment. It can't be measured against a definition found in a dictionary. Humility can only be gained when we transition to the true self that God intended. People in recovery call it "right sizing." Simply put, it means that we become honestly comfortable in our own skin.

Overblown narcissism and extreme self-hatred are just two sides of the same coin. Neither gives any credit to God. One side says that I am superior to others and have no need for God, while the other tells me that I'm so worthless that even God wouldn't love me. It may surprise you to learn that both are egocentric. Thankfully, most people do not exemplify this extreme behavior, but almost all have leanings in one direction or the other. Balance is acquired spiritually the same way that a small child learns to stand and walk on their own. It takes persistence, practice and plenty of falling.

The order of these 12 transformative steps is no accident. They are like the rungs of a ladder that we use, one at a time, to extricate ourselves from the abyss of self. If we go through life on a planet with 6 billion other people living on it and never feel truly connected because of a distorted view of self, have we really lived at all? Certainly not the way that God intended.

The removal of our character defects is something God does so that we may be of service to Him and others. It's not to make us feel better. If we are ambivalent about the fact that this healing makes us useful to His purpose alone, then we're not humble at all. The ego is still trying to put itself first.

FINDING PURPOSE AND POWER

Humility and humiliation are not the same thing. It's important to be clear about the difference. Humility allows us to view ourselves and others as equals. We see ourselves as no better or worse than anyone else. As God's children, we are good with who we are, have a positive self-image and are willing to have Him outfit us with the tools necessary to complete the tasks that He assigns.

The God of my understanding has nothing to do with humiliation and degradation of people. There is no love found in the act of humiliating another person or myself. Addiction is that type of debasement. God wants me to stand up straight and represent a higher standard while gratefully following His lead.

In this step we "Humbly ask Him to remove our shortcomings." That means we need to pray. It's important to ask God for help. Our connection through prayer gives us much more than a pathway for communication. Think of it as a power cord for your cell phone. Without plugging into a power source, the phone will eventually become unusable. Without prayer, so will we become the same way. Lack of power is the great dilemma for all people, whether they are the head of a large multinational corporation, or the homeless person that begs on the street.

Prayer is a powerful tool. It changes lives in unimaginable ways. With respect to character defects, we ask that God remove what He finds objectionable, so that we may be useful. The following prayer is something AA's refer to as the 7th Step prayer and like the 3rd Step prayer, this can be found in the Big Book.

> *My Creator, I am now willing that you should have all of me, good and bad.*
>
> *I pray that you now remove from me every single defect of character which stands in the way of my usefulness to you and my fellow man.*
>
> *Grant me strength, as I go out from here, to do your bidding.*

This simple prayer works because it is devoid of selfishness. Making ourselves to be of service to God in all things is a lofty goal, but each time we use prayers like this one, we are reminded that we need to stay focused. God knows just how to use us and our character defects to maximum effect. When we allow God to fit us into life in that way, our impact on others has maximum depth and weight.

Chapter 8

STEP EIGHT...WE MADE A LIST OF ALL PEOPLE WE HAD HARMED AND BECAME WILLING TO MAKE AMENDS TO THEM ALL

BROTHERLY LOVE

The work we have done so far has been directed inward. Through inventory and self-searching, we've come to grips with the totality of our lives to this point. We've given ourselves over to God as we understand Him, or at least become willing to believe in a Power greater than ourselves. We've identified our greater character defects and the people we've been resentful toward. We've looked closely at what our part was in everything that has ever happened to us. Through our honest admissions to God and another person, we have been freed from the weight of our secrets. We have recognized the power of God to remove our imperfections as He sees fit. It's good work to be sure, but now it's time to go outside of ourselves and do something with it.

Many would suggest letting bygones be bygones. For our purposes, that just won't do. Making amends to people we have harmed is something that practically nobody looks forward to, but it is absolutely necessary for our spiritual growth.

Before we rush off to throw ourselves at the mercy of people who are currently involved in our life, or those from our past, we need to have a plan. More importantly, we need the conviction to follow through. Remember, we must be willing to make amends with the person that we would least like to see again. This is no time for half-measures. We need the conviction to face every single person that we've hurt.

DOING THE RIGHT THING

As we prepare to make direct amends to these people in the next step, we first need to compile a comprehensive list of anyone who we have harmed physically, emotionally, verbally or financially. We go back through our life, writing down every name we can remember. Using the list of people from our resentment inventory and the people we spoke about in our 5th Step admission should be a good start. It may be very useful to talk about this with our close-mouthed friend.

Amends means much more than saying "I'm sorry." We need a fundamental change in the thoughts and behaviors that led us into the actions that we're now making amends for. Without that change, our pleas for forgiveness are self-serving at best. So becoming ready to make amends goes much deeper than just compiling a list.

Concern for the person receiving the amends is a very large consideration, even if we don't particularly like them. It's not about being a "bigger person". That is just ego. We do it because it is the right thing to do. We put our feelings aside, stand up straight and own up to our part in any discord that stands between us and them.

Ask God for the willingness to follow through, even if we swore that we would never talk to that person again. In order to go to these people, we must be willing to forgive them before we make the approach. If we haven't forgiven them first, the chances of either party getting any relief or freedom from the encounter becomes minimal at best.

The power of forgiveness is seriously underestimated in modern times. Maybe it has always been. Even for those of you who are familiar with the Christian Bible, you may be surprised to learn that Jesus illustrated the concept of forgiveness more than any other. His position was considered radical then and it still is today. It seems that although his message was heard, it was never heeded.

Jesus appeared in human form so that other human beings could relate to him. He never ran around beating his chest while proclaiming that he was God. He never asked anyone to worship him. What he did was implore people to follow him. In other words, he led by example of what it meant to by fully human, but dedicated in service to our God. His message of hope was good news to all people, not just Jews or those who were about to become the first Christians. He transcended organized religion, including all people in his message of love and tolerance. The power of forgiveness was his main message.

It is important to remember that the person we make amends to will surely remember things differently than we do. That is why it's so important to ask questions when we are in their company. Ask how they remember the incident(s). Ask if there is anything that you don't remember. We get so wrapped up in ourselves sometimes that we offend people without ever recognizing it.

NOBODY SAID IT WOULD BE EASY

Fear is never justification for putting off a deserved amends indefinitely. On the other hand, we should never go in front of anyone if we are unable to be honest, humble and willing to make things right, no matter what that may entail. God presents us with opportunities to make amends at the proper time. It's our job to be ready when those moments arise. We stand tall with purpose and conviction. We are not aloof and distant, nor do we grovel and beg. We simply take responsibility for our actions.

Due to geographic problems, it may not always be convenient to meet face to face with everyone on our list. Phone calls and letters can be used to reach out, but it's preferable to do amends in person whenever possible. Making the effort to go and see someone and look them in the eye goes a long way when it comes to melting the ice. It's a sure sign that you care and sincerely want to be there. Most people respond well in this scenario.

If money is involved, reasonable reparation can always be made. Making amends to one person can't interfere with your ability to take care of yourself and your family now. Overpromising and then under delivering is an exercise in futility, often resulting in resentment. Do only what you can do. Something is always better than nothing and any reasonable person will understand this.

I feel it necessary to restate the obvious. Before charging out hat in hand, talk with a trusted friend or counselor, someone familiar with skillful amends. What may seem like a good idea to you may actually be a recipe for disaster. There is a time and a place for everything. There are ways to ensure successful encounters and there are ways to make things even worse. Two heads can think better than one. Be a good listener. If you are, you'll know what to say when the time comes.

Most importantly, stay close to your Higher Power before, during and after you begin this process. If you're having particular difficulty with a certain person, ask God for the willingness to go through with it. It may take some time, but with the guidance of an honest heart, you can never go wrong.

Chapter 9

STEP NINE...WE MADE DIRECT AMENDS TO SUCH PEOPLE WHEREVER POSSIBLE, EXCEPT WHEN TO DO SO WOULD INJURE THEM OR OTHERS

JUSTICE

There is a selfish component found in spiritual recovery. It must always begin with us. As I said in the previous chapter, the first seven steps force us to look at ourselves. We are challenged to live on a higher spiritual plane and conduct ourselves accordingly. We are guided by our Higher Power and the sincere desire to live our best possible life. But the process demands more of us for continued growth.

Making direct amends to people we have harmed is a way to balance the scales. By doing this uncomfortable task, we demonstrate the courage, integrity and humility instilled in us by working the previous steps. Remember that action validates everything we've done so far. Only by demonstrating our conviction to walk a different path do we testify to God's love and mercy and His unfathomable power to effect change in the lives of all who seek Him. We do more than talk the talk. We walk the walk.

UPRIGHT AND VIRTUOUS

It takes a big person to stand up and own it when they've wronged another person. It's the unmistakable mark of a spiritually upright man or woman. God rejoices when we honor ourselves by honoring each other.

Until they are put into action, the concepts of patience, tolerance, kindness and love towards our sisters and brothers have no value. In this step, we need to practice all four of them. We often forget that every other person on earth has, or will, struggle with the same fundamental questions that we have. Those who are well-adjusted got that way because they worked at it. Then again, there are plenty who have not. Our amends list will likely consist of both types and should be tailored to fit the person.

There are eight crucial steps before this one, each designed to get us to this point. The time has come to venture out into the "real world" and demonstrate what we've learned with other people. We don't do it for a pat on the back and we don't do it for absolution. Some may never forgive us. We do it because we are compelled to. This is where we get back on a level playing field with every man, woman and child. We show them what we're made of and leave the outcome to God. Getting square with people we have hurt is our business. What they think of us is theirs.

Amends are about healing. Old grudges and ill feelings can be melted away, making possible the renewal of relationships long lost. At the very least, the lines of communication can be opened to the possibility of future reconciliation. I've seen whole families, once torn hopelessly apart, not only come back together, but forge bonds even stronger than before. All it takes sometimes is for one person to step up and own their part in a twisted drama that may have many principle actors. Someone has to go first.

THE REWARD OF ACTION

You will begin to see a new freedom and a new happiness appear in your life. The steps are designed to liberate us from the bondage of self. There are very few things in life scarier than becoming stuck in your own head. Sometimes it can feel like there is no escape. But the steps offer you a way out. They also release you from other people and the expectations surrounding your control issues. Keeping your own side of the street clean is its own reward.

You will not regret the past or wish to shut the door on it. Working the steps to the very best of your ability will help you gain perspective. The past, with all of its ups and downs, brought you to this very moment and the opportunity to change your life. Your past is valuable to your continued development, even if you may not think so right now. Denying your past is tantamount to killing a piece of yourself. Be grateful for the opportunity to see who you are. You'll find that one truth leads to another.

After all, your truth led you here.

You will comprehend the word serenity and you will know peace. If you've ever felt like the problems in your life never end and that you would do almost anything to have a moment to yourself, then this particular promise may be worth the price of admission all by itself! There are levels of serenity waiting to be discovered. It begins with a feeling of calm when the world around you is on tilt.

Pursuing what serenity means to you through prayer and meditation will help you achieve it. Although just getting 10 minutes to yourself at the end of the day might seem like peace, it pales in comparison to what this promise describes. True peace is a life without unhealthy fear. God knows no fear and when you choose to walk beside Him, you're unhealthy and unreasonable fears begin to dissipate.

No matter how far down the scale you have gone, you will see how your experience can benefit others. You've learned things in your life from other people and by trial and error. You can learn something from everyone you meet, even if it's a lesson in what not to do. Your experiences are just as valuable. There is someone who needs what you have to offer. God has a knack of putting those people in your life when you least expect it. Be vigilant and when the people who need you appear, share honestly with them. Paying it forward is rewarding for both parties.

Any feelings of uselessness and self-pity that you may have will disappear. The fastest way to get out of your own head and away from self-serving behavior is to be helpful to other people. Volunteering your time, lending your experience and expertise, or just committing a random act of kindness each day while expecting nothing in return, will give you the encouragement to do even more. It feels good to help someone else. You may find that being of service helps you even more than it does them!

You will lose interest in selfish things and become interested in others. Self-seeking will slip away. The need to dominate others begins to fall away. This is a good indicator that your spiritual connection is getting stronger. Sometimes people can surprise you. If you're an active listener, you may discover that the person sitting across from you is a whole lot more than you thought they were. When you care more about the welfare of others than you do about satisfying selfish wants, magic begins to happen. Paradoxically, the more you do for others, the better YOU begin to feel!

Your entire attitude and outlook upon life will change. In a negative world, a positive attitude is a refreshing change. Keeping an upbeat outlook and attitude is a choice. The steps will influence you to make these positive and life-affirming choices. You reap what you sow. You will find that when you put positive energy out, more often than not, you'll receive positive returns.

Fear of people and of economic insecurity will leave you. There is a big difference between fear and healthy respect. When you do God's will and put your life in His care, fear starts to lose its grip on you. Early in the steps, you saw the importance of placing your dependence on Him rather than on other people. They only have power over you if you give it to them. When "doing the next right thing" becomes second nature, providing for yourself and your family will become less stressful. You'll always get assistance in having your needs met because God really does help those who help themselves!

You will intuitively know how to handle situations that used to baffle you. The 12 Steps are not a plan of thinking. They are a plan of action. By repeating estimable actions again and again, they gradually become second nature. Honesty really is the best policy. The truth really will set you free. Faith really can move mountains. Problems become nothing more than an opportunity for you to be a living example of God's power to change us. When in doubt, ask God for direction. Like the old saying goes, "When the student is ready, the Teacher will appear!"

You will suddenly realize that God is doing for you what you could not do for yourself. When you finally make the decision to surrender completely to your Higher Power and join the winning side, you will enter a 4th dimension of existence, the likes of which you can't even imagine. The ordinary will become extraordinary. You will begin to see everything differently. Life will take on an entirely new meaning to you and you will, maybe for the first time ever, clearly see the path to your best possible life! I PROMISE!!!

These are the promises of the 12 Steps and the payoff for the work. They have been coming true in the lives of people for a very long time. They will come to fruition in your life also, providing that you are willing to do this work.

DISCRETION IS THE BETTER PART OF VALOR

As it was originally written, the step says that we "Made direct amends to such people wherever possible, except when to do so would injure them or others." It's important that we don't overlook the part about injuring the intended party, or anyone else. Throwing another person under the bus in order to save ourselves does not constitute amends. Honesty devoid of compassion is just cruelty.

Let's say that a person has had an affair and their conscience is killing them. Should they tell the spouse about it if that person has no idea that an affair has ever taken place? There is no easy answer to that. We do not have the right to hurt an innocent party in order to relieve our burden of guilt. In a case like this, it may be necessary to do a "living amends." We should definitely talk about what we've done with someone. Hopefully we've already admitted this in Step 5. Living amends simply mean that we ask God for help with our problem. How would we feel if the roles were reversed? It's a fair question.

What if the spouse knows about the affair and wants to know the name of the person we were involved with? Naming names just makes things worse. We need to reassure our spouse that the affair is over and that we will take the necessary steps to insure that it won't happen again. Redirecting rage towards another person to avoid being fully accountable is more than just bad form. It can also be deadly. Jealousy never has a good ending.

There are countless examples of ways to do this step wrong. The founders of AA learned this lesson the hard way. They realized that not everyone should hear everything. The point I want to make here is that we really need to have a plan as to how you are going to accomplish this step. Again, I'm convinced that if there is any doubt about what to say, it should be run by a neutral party first. Objectivity leads to insight and wisdom. Remember, the goal is to see both sides get relief.

Words can hit some people harder than an atomic bomb. Once vocalized, the things that we say can never be taken back. In these days of texting and social media, this fact has become even more apparent. I harken back to a wise old saying..."If you don't have anything nice to say, don't say anything at all." Now those are words to live by.

Be careful when you make amends and have a clear understanding of why you are doing it. Allow your Higher Power to remove the fear from your heart, then make things right. Learn from your mistakes and aspire to something better. Rejoice in knowing that doing the right thing is its own reward.

Carter Francis

Chapter 10

STEP TEN...WE CONTINUED TO TAKE A PERSONAL INVENTORY AND WHEN WE WERE WRONG PROMPTLY ADMITTED IT

PERSEVERANCE

Step work makes it clear that time is a valuable commodity. Yesterday is history and tomorrow is a mystery. All we really have is today. Learning to live in the moment fully, taking nothing for granted, may be the greatest gift of all. Being accountable on a daily basis keeps us grounded and living in the moment.

Personally, the steps have given me some clear direction and a path that I am only too willing to follow. I often say that I have only one real goal for my life. That is to allow God to make me just a little bit more in the image He has in mind for me each day. I will consider my life a success if, on the day that I die, I have become the best man that I can possibly be, honoring my Higher Power for the gift He has given me. I will go to any lengths in order to make that happen.

THE ONGOING STEPS

People who are committed to this spiritual journey understand that the steps really never end. They continue to reshape us for as long as we allow them to work in us. This particular step is one that we do each day moving forward. It keeps us accountable to ourselves, others and God. We learned when we did inventory in Step 4 that when junk builds up and is allowed to remain, it slowly takes over and leaves no room for the things in life that are worthwhile. This step reminds us to be vigilant and keep our own house clean.

Before we go to bed at night, we need to think back on our day and the things that we've done. Hopefully there will be little or nothing weighing us down. But if there is, we make a point of dealing with it right away. Nobody is perfect. Although we work hard on becoming the best person we can each day, we will never be perfect either. The principle of perseverance simply means that we are willing to hold to the course of action that we've embarked upon and never let up. Our goal is simply progress. If we aren't moving forward, we are losing ground. There is no more room in our lives for stagnation and ambivalence.

LIVING A QUALITY LIFE

Personal inventory gives us the opportunity to live each day without excessive baggage. Life on life's terms is difficult enough. God aids us in streamlining our lives, eliminating the resistance that saps our energy and holds us back. We get out of our own way and become free men and women again. We become extremely efficient and stop wasting time.

The price that we pay for our newfound freedom is accountability. Putting out the "fires" of our own making is tiresome. But by staying vigilant, we finally begin to understand the futility of taking one step forward and two steps back. Since negative consequences can only be caused by negative actions on our part, we stop reinforcing the character defects that lurk in the shadows of bad behavior. When we do slip up, as humans inevitably do, we deal with it promptly. Put simply, if you don't want to do an amends again, then don't do the behavior!

Living a purposeful life and following God's will for us inevitably leads us to estimable actions. So when we look back on our day, we need to recognize the good things that we've done. There is deep satisfaction derived from living a spiritually directed life. Approval for our good deeds, although reassuring, is no longer necessary. We, along with our Higher Power, know the good we have brought into the lives of others. In the end, that's all that really matters.

The spiritual journey lasts for a lifetime. We need to develop a routine that works. Daily contact with our Higher Power is absolutely essential. I'm an early riser and always have quiet time in the morning to pray and meditate. I try never to go to bed without first thanking God for another day, identifying moments that I could have handled differently and letting the people close to me know that I love them. I pray for the welfare of all of my friends and family and the ability to be a good example in the day to come.

Chapter 11

STEP ELEVEN...WE SOUGHT THROUGH PRAYER AND MEDITATION TO IMPROVE OUR CONSCIOUS CONTACT WITH GOD AS WE UNDERSTOOD HIM, PRAYING ONLY FOR KNOWLEDGE OF HIS WILL FOR US AND THE POWER TO CARRY THAT OUT

SPIRITUAL AWARENESS

"The spiritual life is not a theory. We have to live it." These words from AA's famous Big Book succinctly describe the 12 Step program of recovery. The obvious question then becomes how to accomplish that. We do it one day at a time, the best that we can. It also means that we start letting God drive the bus. We do the legwork and leave the decision making to Him. The only way that we can receive His instruction is through prayer and meditation.

This step is very specific about "praying only for knowledge of His will for us and the power to carry that out." In the simplest possible terms, this just means that we ask for guidance in doing the next right indicated thing. It's not always easy. Selfish prayers have been around since we started walking on two legs. Unselfish prayer on a daily basis takes practice.

I was always terrible at New Year's resolutions. I don't think I ever kept one promise I made to myself on January 1st. But after I got sober, I vowed to improve my conscious contact with God on a daily basis by doing this step. Every year I reaffirm my commitment to continue this on New Year's Day. It's a resolution that I've kept, and it's changed my life. Feel free to make it your own.

It takes plenty of discipline to work the 12 Steps. The power of spiritual connection has been a revelation thus far, but there is no such thing as too much prayer and meditation. We need to set the goal of becoming more God-conscious each day. We accomplish this through practice and gradually draw closer to Him. As our faith deepens, the nature of our prayers begins to change. We ask God to direct our thoughts to what He would have us do, and pray for the necessary power to carry out His wishes. The answers will come to us, as long as we are open to receive them.

When our desire to do God's will supersedes the desire to serve our own selfish wants, we know that the process is taking hold in our lives. But it takes a lifetime of practice to make it second nature. Defeating the destructive aspect of our ego is no small task. We are constantly checking our motives and exposing the darkest places of our hearts to the Light. Remember that our objective is to become aware of God's plan and to implement it as effectively as possible. We can't do that if we put ourselves first.

PRAY THROUGH THE DAY

If you are a person that feels uncomfortable with the ritual of prayer and meditation, here's a suggestion. Long, wordy prayers sound nice, but short, simple ones are just as effective. On the way to work, say something like *"God save me from anger. Thy will be done."* If the traffic is bad enough, it may be even more appropriate! When facing a perplexing situation, take a minute and silently ask what He would have you do. Since God knows everything about you, there are times when all you have to say is *"God help me."* There is no need to explain why...He already knows.

Many people are confused about the nature of meditation. "To think deeply about; reflect upon; contemplate." This is the dictionary description. That works, but what many people in recovery, including myself, have found is that meditation is a time to quiet the mind and listen. Many people attempt to empty their minds out completely. After all, it's our broken "thinkers" which cause all the problems, right? Maybe it's not such a bad idea to give it a rest occasionally!

There are times when God will communicate directly with you through other people. Someone will speak up about a subject that is on your mind, but haven't mentioned to them. This is no mistake. God really does work in mysterious ways! There is an old saying advising that, "When the student is ready, the Teacher will appear." God is always present in our lives and ready to help. People are put in our life for a reason, not by accident.

Keep in mind that this is a process. We are far from perfect. This step encourages us to improve our conscious contact with God. So try not to be hard on yourself if you fall short of the mark on occasion. There is no sin in falling down. The only sin is choosing to stay down. Keep trying and don't give up. You are never alone when your connection to Him is intact.

Carter Francis

Chapter 12

STEP TWELVE...HAVING HAD A SPIRITUAL AWAKENING AS THE RESULT OF THESE STEPS, WE TRY TO CARRY THIS MESSAGE TO ALCOHOLICS AND TO PRACTICE THESE PRINCIPLES IN ALL OF OUR AFFAIRS

SERVICE

God asks that we show mercy to others, just as He has to us. There is always someone out there who needs help. It is our responsibility to do what we can when the need arises. It's become far too easy to sit back and say, "It's OK. Someone else will do it...or, I have enough problems of my own." Scarier still is the ambivalence towards the suffering of others, accompanied by a complete and total lack of empathy.

We've collectively forgotten the old idea of "walking a mile in another person's shoes." The tendency is to make snap judgements on people, leaving no room for the truth. The world today is largely filled with people in service to self. The 12 Steps teach us that positive change is possible. We allow God to transform us, then we demonstrate His grace through our interaction with others. We change the world one person at a time when we provide a positive example to follow.

Nothing we do will get us out of our own heads faster than working with other people in a service capacity. Making a difference in the life of another person is simply the best thing we can do. The type of service that I'm eluding to is free of charge, and free of expectation on our part. We do it because we can. You'll make a difference and feel wonderful all at the same time. That's a win- win.

I saw a news clip of Jimmy Carter and his wife hammering nails on a build site the other day. They've worked for Habitat for Humanity for decades. The man has been on this earth for over 90 years and has done just about every possible thing that a man could do in one lifetime. He was an Admiral in the U.S. Navy, Governor of Georgia and President of the United States. He's earned the right to enjoy his last years any way he sees fit. Yet he and his wife are routinely seen volunteering at build sites, or wherever they are needed. He might not have been the greatest President in the history of our country, but you will have a hard time finding a better human being that ever occupied that office.

Caring about other people requires more than verbalization. Action is what really makes the difference in their lives. For alcoholics, this step gives clear direction...and a promise. It implies that if we've done each of the previous 11 Steps to the best of our ability, we will have had a spiritual awakening by now. We are then encouraged to carry our message of hope to others who want to recover and who need to experience a spiritual rebirth in order to do so.

Finally, it mandates that we practice these 12 principles in every aspect of our lives. The 12 Step program, as you have no doubt seen, is a spiritual program. Ultimately, it encourages us to solve all of our problems on a spiritual basis.

YOU CAN MAKE A DIFFERENCE

Obviously, working with alcoholics and addicts is best left to those who have been down that path. But you no doubt have struggled with something during your life and that qualifies you uniquely to help someone who is struggling with that same problem. Being of service has no limitations. You need only follow your heart. It will always lead you towards the next right thing to do. The spirit of giving freely is divinely inspired.

The challenge of the 12 Step program really lies in the final few words of the step, where we are given the instruction "to practice these principles in all of our affairs." That means we live it. For us, the principles of Honesty, Hope, Faith, Courage, Integrity, Willingness, Humility, Brotherly Love, Justice, Perseverance, Spiritual Awareness and Service are not just words on a page. They are the guideposts of our life, and the more that we reinforce them each day, the more they become a part of us.

Human beings are not now, nor will they ever be, perfect. As the original text of Alcoholics Anonymous proclaims, "We are not saints." Keeping our expectations reasonable and our goals attainable is the key. "We claim spiritual progress rather than spiritual perfection." So do the best that you can. Be honest and true to yourself along the way.

With your Higher Power to guide you, you can never get lost!

Chapter 13

SPIRITUAL EXISTENCE IN MODERN TIMES

I often wonder what Bill Wilson and the other early members of AA would think if they could see what AA looks like today. Their original text is still used and the 12 Steps have become known worldwide as the most effective way to arrest alcoholism and addiction. But they would be disappointed in the fact that recovery rates have declined from the early days of the organization. Their comparisons would inevitably show that there are two reasons why. People simply don't interact with each other like they used to and the spirit of service in the "me" generation doesn't support long-term recovery.

Nations were in dispute and fought with each other in the first half of the 20th century just as they do today. Stock markets rose and fell. Immigrants clamored to get into the country. Power and elitism separated the wealthy from the working class. But there is one fundamental difference that is clearly visible. People are becoming more and more disconnected from each other. Ironically, this comes at a time when mass communication has never been easier.

It's not that we don't communicate...we do. Somebody is saying something about someone on Twitter or Facebook 24 hours a day. Cheap cell phones and cell service have made it possible for most people to carry a tool for mass communication right in their pocket or purse. There again, most would rather text than actually talk. When you sit in a coffee shop, or walk down the street, nobody is talking to each other. They all have their head down, focused on their master, talking at each other. If you believe for a second that this mentality doesn't carry over into every aspect of life, then you need to wake up.

You could be standing next to someone who could change your life on the subway commute to work. The person of your dreams might walk into Starbucks while you sit staring at your laptop and you'll never know it. Online dating has replaced the way that people have met each other since the origins of man in just the last ten years! The point is this...we're losing the ability to really connect with each other in a way that actually matters...face to face and interpersonally. We are becoming more desensitized to the power of human interaction and the more that we continue to depersonalize each other, the more we drift apart. It seems that everyone is just too busy to talk. With all of that "busy" going on, where does God fit in? The last time I checked, the new spelling for God was A-P-P-L-E. Don't get me wrong. I own an iPhone, and I love it, but it will never fascinate me as much as a grove of trees, or a snow-capped mountain range, or a hummingbird, or the way that my granddaughters look at me.

TURNING BACK THE CLOCK

I sit in amazement sometimes, pondering the events that have taken place just in my lifetime. The drive to achieve has always spurred us on, but nothing can be done alone. When people come together not only in great numbers, but in spirit, almost anything becomes possible. We need each other. Our planet really isn't that big and the amount of resources and food available to all people is limited, although you would never know it judging by the amount of waste that takes place, especially here in America.

What do you think would happen if a modern family was suddenly transported back to 1935? Think about what life would look like to them. Initially, our time travelers would be looking around in disbelief and I'm sure that there would be plenty of complaining about the lack of distractions...no TV, no computers, no cell phones, no video games. And there would be fear. But before too long they would begin to interact, right about the time they realized that all they truly have is God and each other. They would talk and become closer.

Seeing Light in the Cracks

I grew up in a small, rural town in northwestern Colorado. The town survived on ranching and tourism. Skiing dominated the landscape for about half of each year. There was no cable or satellite TV in the 60's and early 70's. We only had reception for two of the national television networks. We had a rotary telephone. Families were intact for the most part, everyone knew everyone and you could sleep safely at night if you didn't bother to lock your doors, which most people didn't. The churches were busy on Sunday. Kids recited the Pledge of Allegiance before school started each day and played together, outdoors mostly, after school. In all my years growing up there, I can only remember a couple of kids who were overweight. Although not perfect, life was pretty good.

There were no fast food chains in my little town. People ate meals at home with their families. If they did go out for dinner on special occasions, they did it together. Saying Merry Christmas didn't get you sued, it only got you a warm greeting in return. I guess we didn't know what we were missing…

I remember being 8 years old and watching as American astronauts walked on the moon in 1969. They flew there on a rocket as tall as a skyscraper. Today I really understand the magnitude of what all of those people at NASA did in order to achieve that goal. It was a massive team effort fueled by a common dream, impeccable math that was performed on a slide-rule and engineering and manufacturing on a scale never before seen. It's quite astonishing, considering that the computing power of the onboard computers used in the Apollo missions was less than what you would find on an iPad today. It took people, working together at their very best, in order to accomplish this monumental task not once, but six times over a three year period.

FINDING WHAT WE REALLY NEED

Love is the only necessary ingredient for living a good life. Love is impossible without other people and an absolute necessity with them. God gave us human form with the knowledge that love would manifest itself in our lives. His love for us overflows and is justified only when we return it. Since God lives in each of us, honoring each other is also a way of honoring Him. It's time we get refocused on the things that matter. It's not my job to tell you what those things are. It's up to you to uncover them for yourself. But I can promise you with full confidence that what matters most is not the next generation of smartphones, or a car that can drive itself.

For all people, the big problem in life is lack of power. As much as we try to convince ourselves that we are in control, we all KNOW at an instinctual level that we are incredibly vulnerable and that our very existence balances on a razor's edge. The earths' atmosphere, ozone layer and magnetic field are the only things standing between us and immediate death. Our lives, or the lives of our loved ones, can be snuffed out in an instant. Not one person can be 100% certain of what is going to happen tomorrow. As far as human life goes, there are no sure things. So we need power just to get up and live, to face the temporary and uncertain nature of our lives and the fact of our own mortality.

Where do we get that needed power? It sure can't be bought at a store or borrowed from another person. It actually lies at the center of who we are, where we came from and what we innately know to be true. It's the personal relationship that we have with our Creator, the only relationship that has always and will always be there for us. Nobody is born without it. We just need to be awakened to its presence.

The 12 Steps have flourished, not because they were revolutionary ideas, but because they strike at the core of what it means to be fully human yet spiritually motivated. One person helping another helps us all. The ideas promulgated by the steps are as old as man. Patience, tolerance, kindness and love can soften even the hardest heart. They can bridge the gap between any two people, no matter how different their circumstances may seem. But they are concepts embraced only by people who are in touch with their inner spirit. The true "unfortunates" live superficial lives, rising and falling at the whim of the artificial world which they occupy. True happiness, joy and serenity can never be found in the bubble of vanity, selfishness and self-loathing.

There is a better way. At one time, I was convinced that I could find the answers on my own, doing exactly as I pleased along the way. All I really did was scare the daylights out of the people who loved me, tarnish the good name I once had, destroy my own self-image and commit what I consider to be the worst sin of all...wasting time. The spiritual life was offered to me decades ago and I turned my nose up at it. It sounded boring to a guy who was trying to cram as much "living" into life as humanly possible. I didn't want to get cheated out of anything, so I tried almost everything. I found out exactly what pain, unhappiness and desperation felt like. That's exactly where "doing it my way" took me. I left God behind when I left home, full of pipe dreams, with a belief that people in their 30's or older were washed up and stupid. It was all about me.

Fast forward 35 years or so and I can tell you with certainty that I am happiest and most fulfilled when it's not about me...at all. I have my selfish moments. We all do. I've experienced what we in AA call the fourth dimension of existence as the result of doing the 12 Steps and putting them to work in my life. I like it there. It's quite simply the best space that I've occupied in my life. Selfishness only takes me away from it. So I return each day to the realm of the Spirit. Each time I do, my fear dissipates, my inner peace returns and I make myself useful to Him and to you. It's my best possible life.

Chapter 14

TIME

What is time and why is it important? Time, not mathematics, is the true measure of all things. As humans, our lives amount to mere nanoseconds when compared with the age of the universe which we occupy and the concept of living for billions of years is not even comprehensible. So for most of us, the focus is directed at much smaller segments of time...the days, months and years of our lives.

The value of even one minute for a person with a life span of 80 years can't be overestimated. Our lives are finite and fragile. There is a beginning and an end. There is no guarantee of just how long it will last. The enlightened mind understands that time is too precious to waste. So how do we maximize it?

First, we should examine what would constitute a waste of time. To some, reading this book, or any book for that matter, may seem like a lousy way to spend a couple of hours. For others, anything not work related could be considered invaluable. There may be as many opinions on this subject as there are people. Each person assigns time value based upon their likes and dislikes.

Here's what I know for myself. If I spend time worrying about what other people think of me, or if I obsess over the mistakes of others and the fact that the world doesn't run the way I think it should, then I've surely wasted it. Simply put, outcomes aren't my job. They aren't yours either.

Thought and contemplation have great value, but only when followed up with the accompanying action. And make no mistake about it, estimable action is never a waste of time. From a spiritual development perspective, there may actually be no better use of time.

So the questions become clear. What do you spend time on and is it really working for you? Will your life be measured only by the amount of years that you lived, or will you be remembered for the impact, either positive or negative, that you had in the lives of others? Are you living your best possible life each day, or are you wasting your time doing the same old thing? Just remember...nothing changes if nothing changes.

There is no perfection in the physical universe, so the idea that we can streamline our lives to a point where not a moment is wasted is foolish. The idea here is to identify how we can maximize our positive effectiveness in life and be happy at the same time.

SOMETHING TO THINK ABOUT

In the last chapter, I briefly mentioned the Fourth dimension. I want to talk about that for a bit. Geniuses like Albert Einstein and Stephen Hawking devoted their lives to understanding the mysteries of the universe, specifically the relationship between space and time. In the scientific world, time occupies the fourth dimension. In Alcoholics Anonymous, the fourth dimension should represent the goal of all people who do the 12 Steps.

I wish that Bill Wilson was still alive. I'd like to ask him if "being rocketed into a fourth dimension of existence", as he described it in the original Big Book from 1939, was a concept that he derived from Einstein's Theory of Relativity, which was proven to be correct in the 1920's. Wilson would certainly have known about it, at least on a rudimentary level. But I suspect that there was more at work here...a lot more. He was an extremely smart man. Before alcohol took him down, he had been a military officer in WW1 and a Wall Street executive.

Einstein proved that space and time were malleable, that is, they can be altered. By using shear velocity, we can theoretically slow time down as we approach the speed of light, yet time would remain the same at the point of origination. It's a bit difficult for most people to wrap their head around, but a simple example makes it a bit easier to digest.

Imagine that you could get on a spaceship that could somehow attain near-light speed instantaneously. You could leave earth and go in any direction for a week, turn around and come home, all at speeds over 180,000 miles per second. Although only 2 weeks had passed for you, over 100 years would have passed on earth. Effectively, you would have traveled into the future.

Although possible, this type of time travel will be extremely difficult to attain, given the almost unbelievable speeds that we are talking about and the limitations of the human body. So now I harken back to the belief that we are all spiritual beings having a human experience. Our spirit lives inside us as surely as our heart does, yet it is not visible on an x-ray and couldn't be removed during an autopsy even if it could be found. It doesn't operate under the laws of the physical universe and never has.

I believe that Bill Wilson would almost certainly have figured this out, and he left clues in the Big Book of AA. I think he was convinced that anyone could effectively escape the bonds of time if they allowed God to set their mind and spirit free. I can tell you for a fact that it works.

Consider this. Our spirit (who we are) joined our body when we were born, travelling from God-only-knows-where. It traveled that distance in an instant and remains together with our body during our mortal life to remind us where we came from. Spiritual transformation is like a "Get out of jail free" card. It sets our spirit free to go where our body cannot. In essence, we are relieved of the bondage of self. The 12 Steps are the countdown to launch.

God does not experience time like we do. Neither does the spirit which he put into each of us. When we open ourselves up to God and surrender completely, the part of us which is timeless can connect with Him on His time, at His speed, in His domain. Our prayers are sent via our spirit and are instantaneously received. Remember, the spirit is not bound by any laws other than God's. When our spirit joins with God, time stands still.

Chapter 15

AWAKENING

Having a spiritual awakening implies that our spirit has been asleep. In fact, any dictionary will tell you that to awaken simply means to wake up on our own. But it also says that something else can awaken us. So which is it? It seems like such a simple question, but I don't believe the answer is the same for each person.

The 12th Step says that as a result of doing the steps, we will have had a spiritual awakening. What it doesn't tell us is exactly where, in the course of doing these steps, we will have it. Since we never stop working these steps in our life and spiritual growth has no limit, it makes the journey to our spiritual awakening the actual destination. We will have many spiritual awakenings in our lifetime, provided we are willing to stay the course and grow. If you still need a reason to get onboard, there it is.

A big key to enlightenment has always been willingness. It takes commitment and persistence. We never give up before the miracle happens and when the connection is made, we never stop working to improve it. There can be nothing standing between us and our Higher Power, so we stay vigilant and make sure that our path to Him remains clear.

When we wrap ourselves in the comforting blanket of belief, all sorts of wonderful things begin to happen. We realize, sometimes suddenly, that everything will ultimately be OK. With this giant trump card in our hip pocket, the obstacles that we used to view as virtually insurmountable start looking like nothing more than opportunities to grow. We begin to change from the inside out. Oddly enough, it's other people who notice the fundamental changes taking place in us before we do ourselves.

This is the very essence of spiritual awakening. We die to our old way of life and are reborn into a new one. We may still have the same job and live in the same place. In fact, our physical circumstances may or may not look exactly the same. But the truth for us is that nothing is, or ever will be, the same again! We know this to be true at the very epicenter of our being.

THE FIRST DEATH

Although our souls are immortal, our bodies are not. Acceptance of our mortality is a challenge in the life of every person. This fact is unsettling at best and for some, the impetus for a life dedicated solely towards the gratification of self.

On the other hand, the truly enlightened person realizes how fortunate they are. They understand that God has gifted them with the vision to see where the value in life truly lies. The surly bonds that ensnare the masses pose little threat to them. A higher level of accountability, the willingness to surrender to God's will and service to their fellow man, have simply lifted them up to safer ground.

Before our physical death, we must first die to self, that is, the release of our self-centered, or ego-centric tendencies. It sounds simple enough, but this type of ego is an elusive foe and can take many forms. It is deceptive and will stop at almost nothing in order to perpetuate itself. Left unchecked, these various manifestations of self are the very thing that can ultimately defeat us.

Throughout the main text, I have repeatedly made mention of the importance of surrendering to our Higher Power. This is the final blow of the hammer. To find within ourselves the acceptance of God and what it means to totally surrender to His grace and mercy, is the answer to the unhealthy ego. More importantly and pertinent to you and your life, surrender allows symbiosis with our Creator on an individual basis. The desire to separate from God in order to satisfy hedonistic pleasure and self-gratify decreases to the point of non-importance.

THE ANSWER

My great hope is that you find something here that inspires you to look in the right direction for the answers in your life. There is only one. It is the way of the truth and the light. It is the beacon for all to follow out of darkness, sorrow and pain. It elevates all who embrace it to a higher standard of being. It is the true path to understanding.

Nothing has, or ever will happen, without God. There are plenty of very intelligent naysayers out there who would use the limitations of human thought to confuse you. I harbor no ill feelings towards any of them and neither should you. They are people, like you and I, looking for answers. They have a difficult time believing that there is only one answer for everything and The Answer doesn't explain Himself to us and certainly not when we live in human form.

Many wonder if the answer to all questions will be answered to our satisfaction upon our death. We will all get to find that out for ourselves. That much is certain. I believe that many answers can be found while we're still living, most notably, the best way to maximize this amazing gift of life without jeopardizing our precious soul in the process.

To find God is to find yourself. The obstacles in place in the modern world are many and it's very easy to get distracted or lost. Use the steps as a compass and you'll navigate life just fine, no matter what comes your way. Always be honest with yourself. Forgive when everything inside you screams out to strike back. Make love the only weapon you carry, even when it seems inadequate. Have the courage to break away from everything you may think that you know and seek the truth for yourself. Put your relationship with Him above all else in your life and delight in the joy and peace that comforts you as a result. And finally, give freely of what you've been given.

Chapter 16

OBSERVATIONS

The poet, William Blake wrote: *"The road of excess leads to the palace of wisdom."* I can certainly attest to that. Like a lot of people, I got caught up in the culture of the 80's and the 90's, which extolled the virtues of partying and living beyond ones means. Credit was easily obtainable, sex was readily available and like myself, the people I associated with didn't give a damn about tomorrow. We lived for the moment.

The world was changing drastically at that time and America was on top of it. Gone were the days of understated and unified might that saw the country through WWII and the "Leave it to Beaver" decade of the 50's. The baby boomers broke away from the norm in the 60's and early 70's, paving the way for the kids like myself with their defiant attitude and chants of "Sex, Drugs and Rock n' Roll." Young people stopped going to church, instead preferring to worship at the altar of individuality. It became cool to thumb your nose at the establishment.

Materialism became the new God. An actor became President and forced the Russians to capitulate. America became an empire "superpower" and everyone got stoned and drunk. The disease of "more" took hold, divorce rates moved towards 50% and the "latch key" generation was born.

Old school values and morality were set aside in favor of greed and the glorification of celebrities, whose lives were often more dysfunctional than our own. As world leaders, the American attitude and culture spread around the globe. What you see today is the result. We are beginning to feel the consequences of our actions, or lack thereof, as the case may be.

The world I was born into has changed so much that I hardly recognize it. Although the life I live today is a good one, I haven't forgotten the poor decisions I made or the pain which resulted from them. For me, experience was the best and harshest teacher. The trajectory of my life was plainly visible on the faces of my parents and those who cared for me. Few gave me any chance of surviving to the age I am today, based on the way I lived for so many years. Who could blame them?

I was very unhappy, although you never would have heard me admit it. I'm a disabled veteran and I couldn't drink or drug enough to get rid of the bad thoughts that lived in my head, or the memories that haunt me to this day. I've seen what people are capable of, both good and bad.

I was convinced that I could do things my own way. If there was a God, he didn't want anything to do with me. Pride and ego were my best friends. I lived on an island of my own making. It would have been easy for me to blame alcohol, drugs, ex-wives or armed conflict for all of my problems. But none of those things or people took anything from me...not even alcohol. I gave it all away voluntarily. It's on me.

The greatest gift I have to offer is my experience, strength and hope. When someone turns their life around after hearing my story and identifying with me because of it, we both win. The life that led me to ruin turned out to be my salvation. I received the gift of desperation in great measure. My life in recovery has shown me that my past, as crazy as it was, is the tool I use to help others. Being honest about who I am and how I got here is vital to my life today.

I realize that I'm not unique. There are so many people who struggle with the idea that they are misunderstood or marginalized. The problems that have manifested in the world today are a result of our reactions to these feelings. The people I've met in recovery understand that.

I suspect that grandiosity and inferiority are just two sides of the same coin and can be found in all corners of society, not only in rooms where the 12 Steps are passed along. We are being defeated by our intolerance and an attitude of mass denial.

I wasted plenty of time in my life. I won't be guilty of wasting any more. I'll use my remaining time to help as many people as I can. Writing this book is the next step in my evolution and something that I felt compelled to do. I tried to keep it relatively short and easy to read. I didn't want to be long-winded and "preachy".

It is my hope that this material will provide a spark in you, encouraging you to take stock of your life and make the necessary changes. At the very least, I hope that the book will plant a seed in your heart, which will take hold and grow when the time is right. I have no delusions of grandeur. It took plenty of time and suffering before I finally became teachable. People learn in their own time.

Collectively we've lost our way, and it's time to step back on the path together and make things right. That sounds a bit hokey and naive, but why can't it happen? Celebration of each day that we are fortunate enough to live on this beautiful planet should be second nature, shouldn't it? What's so bad about being alive, especially here in America?

I'm a grandparent now and I can tell you that I have great concern about the kind of world that my three granddaughters will need to navigate as they grow into womanhood. My wish for them is that they treat life as the greatest gift of all and that they never lose the sense of wonder that fills their eyes now. Time goes by so quickly and it is far too precious to waste. I've learned that the best instruction I can give is the example I set for them in the way that I act on a daily basis.

The timing is right for a book like this. People everywhere are solving their disputes and promoting their agendas with guns and bombs. No one seems to know what to do about it. Trust has been replaced by suspicion. Fear is used as a tried and true way of selling everything. It's no wonder that most people are simply overwhelmed by their life and the world they live in.

What I've outlined here is a simple way of life and it has been working for groups of people in recovery for decades. It's not religious in nature. It's spiritual. Imagine a world where people solved *all* of their problems on a spiritual basis each day. Now that would truly be something! The only way to effect change like this is one person at a time...one person helping another.

Start with yourself and your family. The disintegration of the family unit is a major cause of the dysfunction we see today. Go ahead...tell me I'm wrong. It's become acceptable to change spouses like underwear and settle for becoming a part-time parent. Whomever can afford the better lawyer gets the upper hand. NEWS FLASH.......jobs and status and money are not more important than being present for your family!

Children are dependent on us for much more than food and shelter. They look to us for guidance on how to act, what's acceptable and what isn't. The example we set for them is a pattern that they will almost surely follow, for better or worse. So here's a question. Are you the best possible example for your family right now, or is there room for improvement?

Remember the old saying "The family that prays together stays together?" In comparison with the majority of Americans (who don't pray regularly or go to church) this statement is valid. Values and a moral code walk hand in hand with spiritual responsibility.

If you're single and don't have children, think about the company you keep. Like children, peers look to each other to find the limits of acceptability and decorum. Living a spiritually based life will crystalize your circle of friends quickly. Those that choose to stay in a self-centered and addicted lifestyle will sift out of your life like water through a colander. What's left is the good stuff...and that is all you really need.

Reading this book will be a complete waste of time if there is no effort on your part to implement these principles in your life. As with most things, what you receive will directly correlate to what you put in to the process. There is nothing to be lost by trying and the rewards can take you to heights previously thought unreachable. It can happen for you.

You ARE God's child, and He loves you!

About the Author

Carter Francis currently lives in Scottsdale Arizona. Raised in Steamboat Springs, Colorado, Carter joined the U.S. Navy and was in active duty service until November of 1985. After the service, he went back to college and then took a job as an assistant Golf Professional. This was an occupation he pursued for the next 23 years. His life in the golf industry allowed him to travel all over the continental U.S.

He still plays golf when his back allows and he enjoys riding his old Harley. Carter's ultimate joy is helping other alcoholics achieve sobriety. He is very active in a men's Bible Study/Recovery group.

"With the time that I have left on Earth, I will do my best to leave things better than I found them, passing on the information and experience that I always seemed to learn the hard way." ...Carter Francis